ENGLISH EMPIRE
BAFFINS BAY
DAVIS
ARCTICK LAND
NEW NORTH WALES
NEW SOUTH WALES
HUDSONS BAY
TERRA LABRADOR
NEW BRITAIN
NEW FOUND LAND
The Main Bank
False Bank
L. PISCOUTAGAMI
L. TABITIBIS
NEW FRANCE
LAKE SUPERIOR
LAKE HURONS
LAKE ERIE
ct of Land
f Wild Bulls
Cape Cod
SEA OF THE ENGLISH EMPIRE
Bermudas als Summer Islands
THE GOLF OR BAY OF MEXICO
Fort St George
C Florida
BAHAMA ISLANDS
ANTILLES Is
WEST INDIAN SEA
CARIBY ISLANDS
SOTTAVAN Is
YUCATAN
HONDURAS
Tabasco
AIN

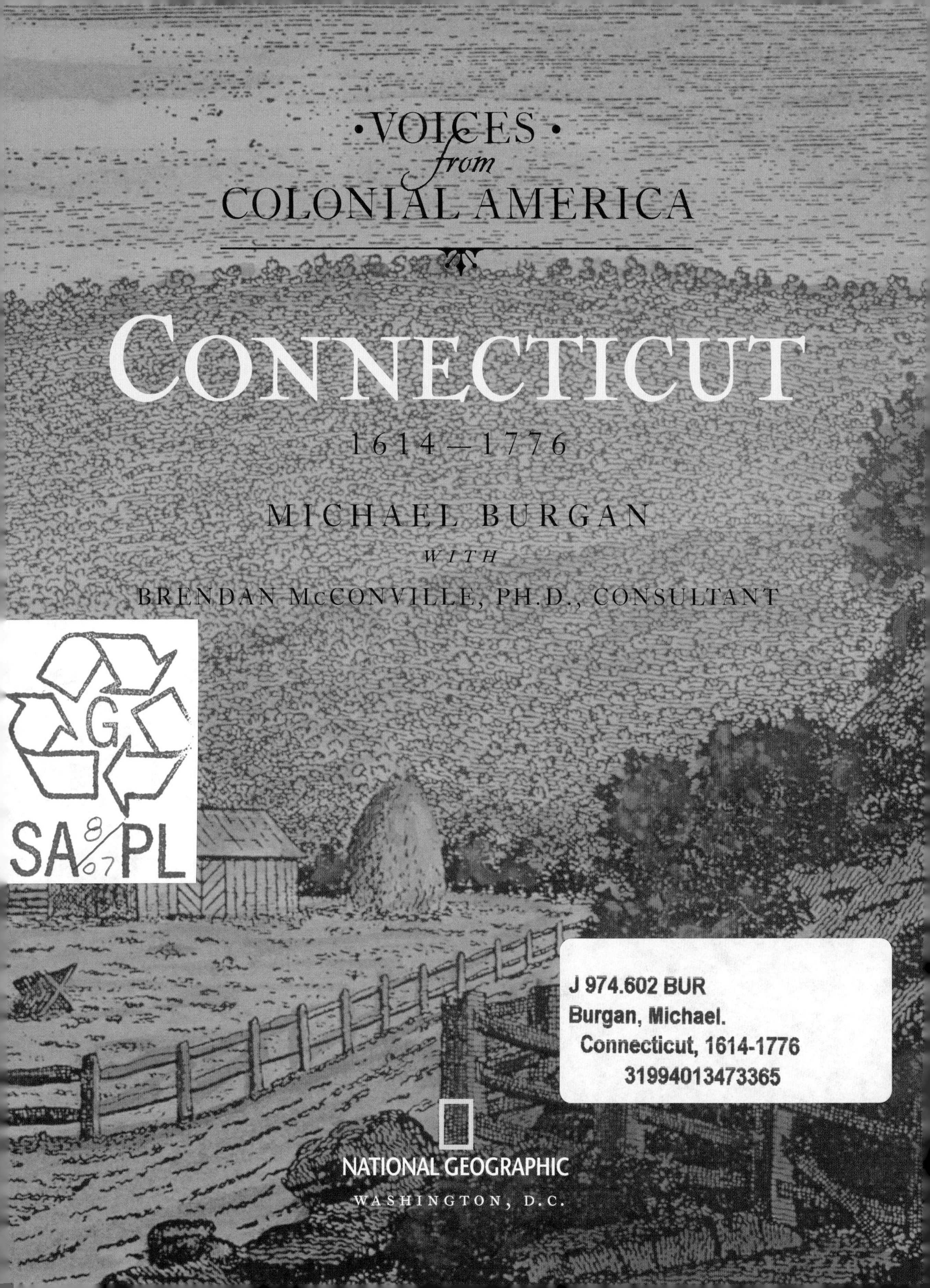

•VOICES• *from* COLONIAL AMERICA

CONNECTICUT

1614–1776

MICHAEL BURGAN

WITH

BRENDAN McCONVILLE, PH.D., CONSULTANT

NATIONAL GEOGRAPHIC
WASHINGTON, D.C.

John M. Fahey, Jr., *President and Chief Executive Officer*
Gilbert M. Grosvenor, *Chairman of the Board*
Nina D. Hoffman, *Executive Vice President, President, Book Publishing Group*

STAFF FOR THIS BOOK

Nancy Laties Feresten, *Vice President, Editor-in-Chief of Children's Books*
Amy Shields, *Executive Editor, Children's Books*
Suzanne Patrick Fonda, *Project Editor*
Robert D. Johnston, Ph.D., *Associate Professor and Director, Teaching of History Program University of Illinois at Chicago, Series Editor*
Bea Jackson, *Director of Illustration and Design, Children's Books*
Jean Cantu, *Illustrations Specialist*
Carl Mehler, *Director of Maps*
Justin Morrill, *The M Factory, Inc., Map Research, Design, and Production*
Rebecca Baines, *Editorial Assistant*
Jennifer Thornton, *Managing Editor*
Connie D. Binder, *Indexer*
R. Gary Colbert, *Production Director*
Lewis R. Bassford, *Production Manager*
Nicole Elliott and Maryclare Tracy, *Manufacturing Managers*

Voices from Colonial Connecticut was prepared by
CREATIVE MEDIA APPLICATIONS, INC.

Michael Burgan, *Writer*
Fabia Wargin Design, Inc., *Design and Production*
Susan Madoff, *Editor*
Laurie Lieb, *Copyeditor*
Jennifer Bright, *Image Researcher*

Body text is set in Deepdene, sidebars are Caslon 337 Oldstyle, and display text is Cochin Archaic Bold.

LIBRARY OF CONGRESS CATALOGING-IN-PUBLICATION DATA
Burgan, Michael.
Connecticut, 1614–1776 / by Michael Burgan.
p. cm. — (Voices from colonial America)
Includes bibliographical references and index.
ISBN-13: 978-1-4263-0068-4 (trade : alk. paper)
ISBN-13: 978-1-4263-0069-1 (library : alk. paper)
1. Connecticut—History—Colonial period, ca. 1600–1775—Juvenile literature. I. Title.
F97.B885 2007
974.6'02—dc22

2007003123

Printed in Belgium

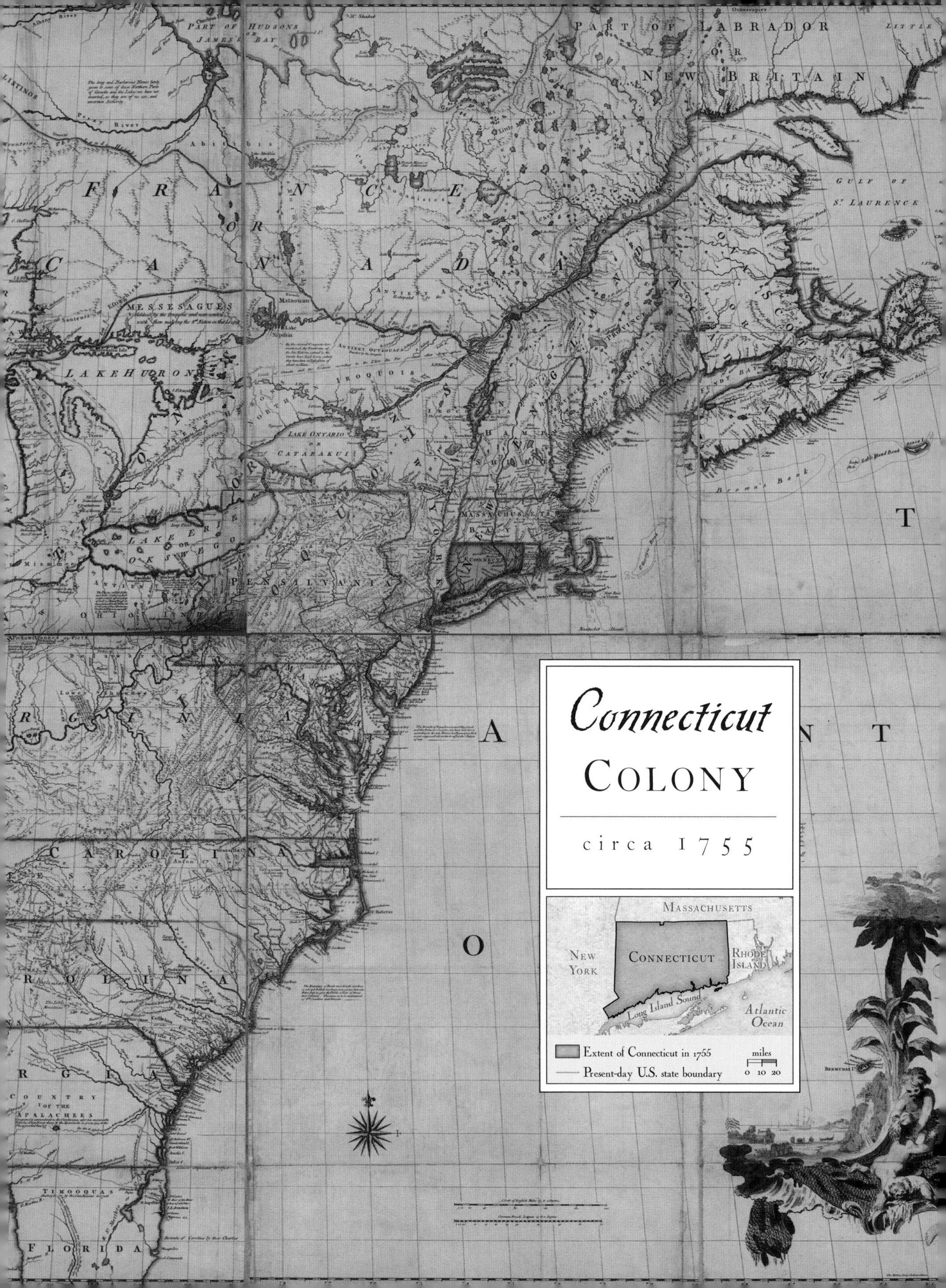
Connecticut
Colony
circa 1755
Massachusetts
New York
Connecticut
Rhode Island
Long Island Sound
Atlantic Ocean
Extent of Connecticut in 1755
Present-day U.S. state boundary
miles
0 10 20
PART OF LABRADOR OR NEW BRITAIN
PART OF HUDSONS OR JAMES'S BAY
GULF OF ST. LAURENCE
LAKE HURON
LAKE ONTARIO OR CATARAKUI
LAKE ERIE OR OKSWEGO
MESSESAGUES
IROQUOIS
MASSACHUSETTS BAY
PENSILVANIA
COUNTRY OF THE APALACHEES
TIMOOQUAS
FLORIDA

INTRODUCTION

by

Brendan McConville, Ph.D.

A Dutch ship sails by *Huys de Hoop* (House of Good Hope), the Dutch fort along the shore of the Connecticut River in present-day Hartford.

The remnants of colonial Connecticut that survive now, in the early 21st century—the shingled houses and stone walls and green fields—speak to a peaceful society of small farming towns and trading communities planted at the mouths of rivers running north and south through the colony. It was a place where farmers and traders worshipped under

OPPOSITE: This historical map, created by John Mitchell in 1755, has been colorized for this book to emphasize the boundaries of the Connecticut colony. The inset map shows the state's present-day boundaries for comparison.

the guidance of Puritan ministers trained at the tiny college in New Haven that has become Yale University.

Connecticut was also a place of warfare and witches, political intrigue, and unbridled commercial activity. This volume in National Geographic's *Voices from Colonial America* series recaptures the drama and importance of Connecticut's colonial history, from the time when Dutch traders first sailed along the north shore of Long Island Sound until the colony rebelled against British rule in 1776. What began as a handful of European settlements sharing the soil with several powerful Native American tribes became, in the 18th century, the site of an astonishing economic and spiritual transformation. Traders and farmers began creating a new social order based on business opportunities, entrepreneurship, and the hope of spiritual salvation.

This early seal of Connecticut uses a design brought over from England in 1639 by Colonel George Fenwick for the Saybrook Colony. When the Connecticut Colony purchased Saybrook, the seal was transferred. The words on the seal translate as "He Who Transplanted Still Sustains," and the supported grapevines probably represent the idea that Connecticut was planted amid a wilderness and grew stronger as the years went on.

Puritans, Mohegans, Pequots, Connecticut Yankees (a term identified with a tradition of excellence and pride in hard work)—all help us, living here in the future, define colonial America, its character and its relationship to the country that emerged after 1776. We cannot think of America before independence without them, or without Uncas, or Thomas Hooker, or John Winthrop, Jr., or John Davenport. All of these people help us put a human face on 300 years of history. In this volume, these groups and individuals become our ambassadors to the complex world that grew along Long Island Sound and the Connecticut River in the 17th and 18th centuries. That society gave birth to "Yankee ingenuity," the inventive, can-do spirit that has propelled America to its position as a global leader. It also gave us Rodger Sherman and the Connecticut Compromise that helped win approval for our Constitution. These contributions made Connecticut a vital crossroads in our development as a nation and as a people.

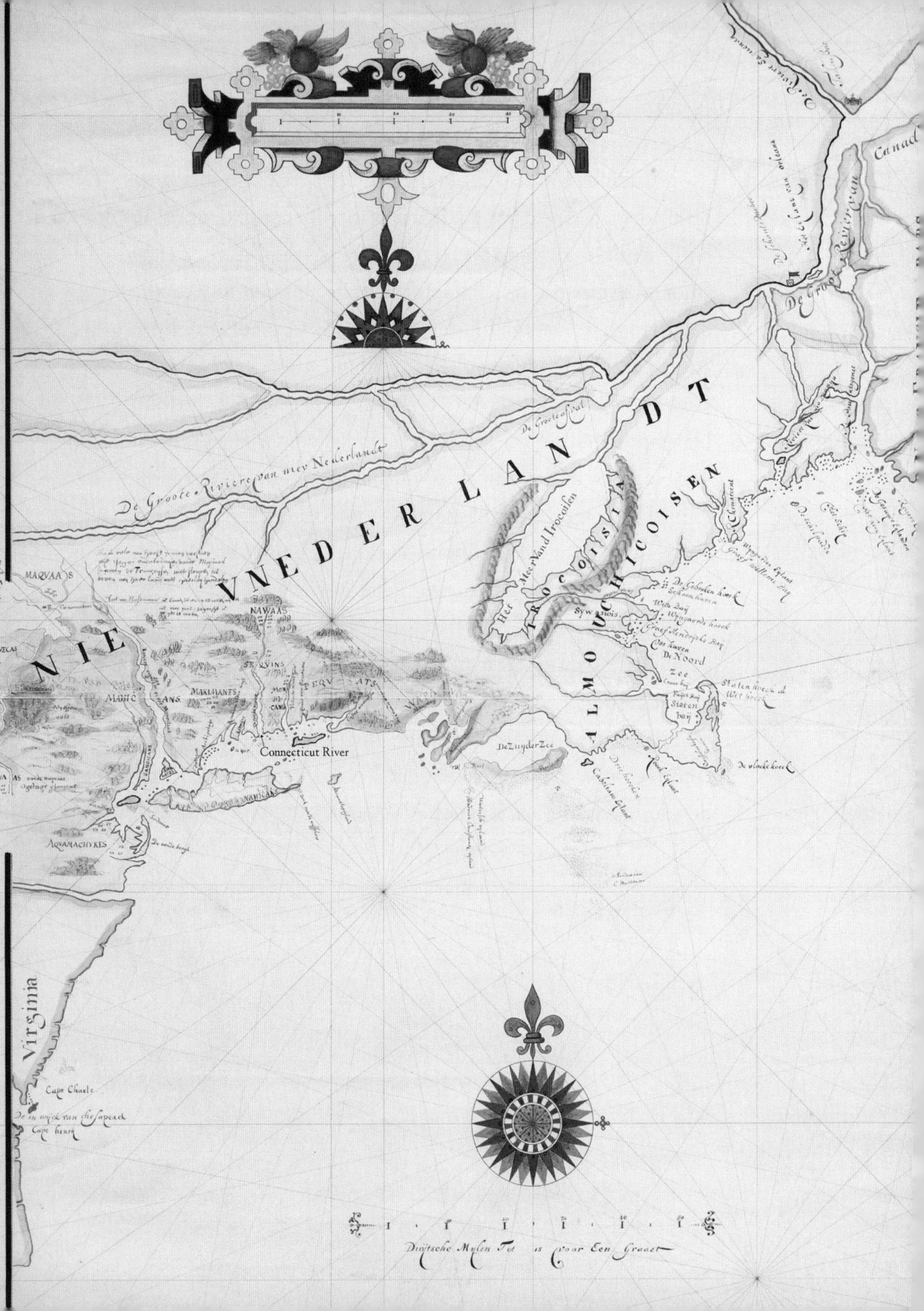

NIE VNEDER LAN DT
IROCOISIA
ALMOUCHICOISEN
De Groote Riviere van niew Nederlandt
De Groote Rivier van
Canad
Het Meer vand Irocoisen
MAQUAAS
SENNECAS
NAWAAS
MAHICANS
MAKIMANES
AQUAMACHYKES
MINQUAAS
Connecticut River
Sywanois
Witte Baij
Cos haven
De Noord zee
Staten hoeck of Wit hoeck
Staten baij
De vlacke hoeck
De Zuyder Zee
Virginia
Cape Charle
De in wijck van chesapeack
Cape henry
Duijtsche Mylen
is Voor Een Graet

CHAPTER ONE

Along the Long Tidal River

DUTCH EXPLORER ADRIAEN BLOCK *travels the river known as Quinatucquet and meets Native Americans who live in the region. The first Dutch fort is built in Connecticut in 1633.*

Early in 1614, Dutch trader and explorer Adriaen Block sailed his ship *Onrust* (*Restless*) from New Netherland's Manhattan Island. Block had come to Manhattan to trade with the Native Americans living there. Now he sought new lands where the Dutch could obtain more of the highly prized beaver skins that the Indians provided.

OPPOSITE: Adriaen Block charted this map during his journey through New Netherland and up the Connecticut River in 1614.

The *Onrust,* barely 45 feet (14 m) long, sailed into what is now called Long Island Sound. Some 90 miles (145 km) east of Manhattan, Block spotted the mouth of a river. He took the *Onrust* about 60 miles (96 km) upstream until rapids in the water halted its progress. Block then returned down the river, which he named the *Versche* (Fresh) River. The local tribes, however, called it the *Quinatucquet,* an Algonquian Indian word that means "long tidal river." That name, with a slightly different spelling, was later used for the river and the land around it. With his explorations, Block became the first European to sail on the Connecticut River, and he made the first contact with the Indian tribes that called Connecticut their home.

The Dutch View OF CONNECTICUT

AFTER SAILING UP THE CONNECTICUT RIVER, Adriaen Block reported that "*the natives there plant [corn], and in the year 1614 they had a village resembling a fort for protection against the attacks of their enemies.*" Several decades later, a history of the Dutch in Connecticut said, "*Connittekock is . . . a very large and beautiful flatland, that daily (usually in the spring) like the Nile Valley is flooded by the rising of the river up to the hills extending along the aforesaid river, and then westward into the countryside.*"

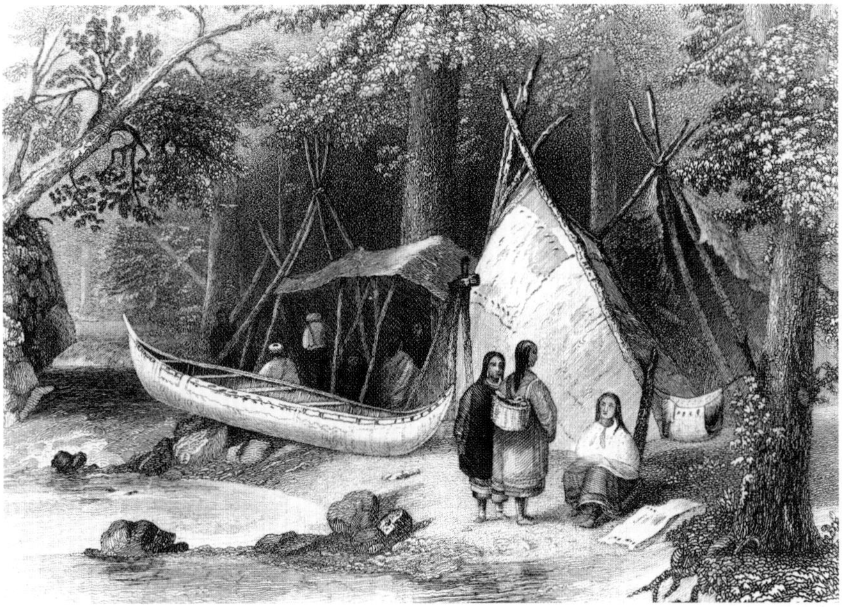

This engraving by W.H. Bartlett shows Algonquian families outside their wigwams along a Connecticut stream.

The Indians of Connecticut

Indians first settled in what would be called Connecticut more than 10,000 years ago. By the time Block arrived, the descendants of those first people had learned how to farm, fish, and make crafts, such as pottery, baskets, and stone tools. The tribes who lived along the shores of the Connecticut River spoke different versions of the Algonquian language. These tribes included the Podunk, the Wongunk, the Sukiaug, and the Hamonassett. Farther east, the main tribes were the Pequot and the Mohegan.

TWO TRIBES, THEN AND NOW

The Mohegan and the Pequot were once a single tribe that came to Connecticut from New York, then separated during the early 17th century. They became bitter enemies in their desire for land and trade with the Europeans. By the end of the 18th century, almost all the members of the two tribes had either left Connecticut or died after contracting diseases spread by Europeans. Starting in the 1980s, the two tribes began to revive in Connecticut. The U.S. government recognized descendants of the Pequot and the Mohegan as independent Indian nations, and both tribes took control of some traditional lands in eastern Connecticut. In 1987, federal laws were passed permitting Native Americans to own and operate casinos on tribal lands. Foxwoods Casino, located in Ledyard, Connecticut, is owned by the Pequot, and the Mohegan Sun, located in Uncasville, is owned by the Mohegan tribe.

The various Connecticut tribes shared a similar lifestyle. Families lived in homes called wigwams, made of wooden poles, bark, and sometimes animal skins. Several villages were usually clustered along a river or other body of water. Women worked the fields, growing corn, beans, and squash, while men hunted and fished. Children helped in the fields and gathered nuts and berries. After the crops were harvested, most tribal bands left their villages for hunting grounds nearby. Their favorite game was white-tailed deer, which they tracked through the snow. The hunters and their families then returned to the farming villages in the spring.

In the hills of western Connecticut lived the Mohawk. They had come from New York, where earlier they had driven the Pequot and the Mohegan from their lands in that region. The Mohawk were one of five tribes that spoke the Iroquois language and formed the Iroquois Confederacy. The Iroquois name for this union was *Hodenosaunee*, which means "people of the longhouse." The Iroquois lived in houses up to 150 feet (46 m) long. The buildings were made of bark and had curved roofs. As many as 12 families might live in one longhouse.

confederacy—a union of people or groups with shared values

Trading with the Indians

On his 1614 trip to what would become the colony of Connecticut, Block saw that the Pequot living near Long Island Sound used polished seashells of purple and white to make beads called *sewan* or wampum. The beads were then strung onto belts. The Dutch learned that the tribes of Connecticut and New York used wampum belts to pay debts or make business deals. In Connecticut, the Dutch traded metal pots, knives, and cloth for the wampum of the Pequot, then traded the wampum for furs from the

Mohawk. The Pequot fought neighboring tribes, such as the Nipmuc and Mattabesic, to protect their control of the Dutch trade.

An 18th-century Algonquian wampum belt is designed with purple shells and three white rectangles, probably representing a wartime alliance of three tribes.

During the early 1620s, the Dutch and the Pequot narrowly avoided armed conflict over Pequot efforts to dominate the wampum trade. The Pequot attacked other Indians who came to trade with the Dutch near what is now Hartford. Jacob Elekens, the head Dutch trader, responded by kidnapping a Pequot chief. Elekens demanded and received a ransom of wampum. The Dutch calmed the situation by replacing Elekens with Pieter Barentsen, who spoke Algonquian and had good relations with the area's tribes. According to official Dutch documents of the day, Elekens's behavior caused the Pequot to distrust *"everyone but Barentsen . . . [who] traded with them . . . in great friendship."*

By 1631, the tribes of the Connecticut River hoped to deal with other European settlers. Wahginnacut, the sachem, or chief, of the Wongunk Indians, traveled to Boston to meet with the officials of Massachusetts Bay, an English colony settled a year earlier. John Winthrop, governor of the colony, reported that Wahginnacut *"was very desirous to have some Englishmen to come plant in his country, and offered to find them corn and give them yearly 80 skins of beaver."*

allies—countries or groups that help each other during a war

The river tribes, however, were not just trying to be friendly. They needed allies in case their disagreements with the Pequot led to war. The Dutch presence in Connecticut was still small, and the English in both Massachusetts Bay and the colony of Plymouth could offer more help if violence erupted.

Winthrop declined Wahginnacut's offer, but word spread to Plymouth about the Indian lands along the Connecticut River. In 1632, Edward Winslow, one of the founders of Plymouth, sailed up the Connecticut River. He reported back to Plymouth that the lands along the river

A founder of Plymouth Colony, Edward Winslow reported the favorable conditions he found in the land along the Connecticut River. This spurred interest in settling Connecticut and led to the development of the first English outpost in the region.

were indeed fertile and that the Indians would be willing partners in the fur trade. In 1633, an expedition led by William Holmes left Plymouth to build a trading post along the river.

By this time, the Dutch had built their first true fort in Connecticut in what is now Hartford. The fort was called *Huys de Hoop*–House of Good Hope. In September 1633, Dutch soldiers readied the fort's two cannon when they saw Holmes's ship head up the river. Jacob Van Curler, the commander of the fort, asked Holmes where he was going. "*Up the river to trade,*" he replied. Van Curler warned that his men would shoot if Holmes did not end his journey. "*I must obey my commands,*" the Englishman insisted. He continued sailing, and the Dutch did not fire.

Although John Winthrop had decided not to send settlers to Connecticut, he did send a ship to explore Long Island Sound and the mouth of the Connecticut River. The vessel then sailed on to Manhattan, where the crew delivered this message to the Dutch governor: "*The King of England has granted the river and country of Connecticut to his own subjects, and therefore desires [that the Dutch should not] . . . build there.*" The English claimed all of New England, based on the explorations of John Cabot in 1497 and John Smith who had named the region in 1614. The Dutch governor replied that the Netherlands had a legal right to the land as well. Although the two sides avoided war, the debate over who owned Connecticut continued for years to come.

First English Settlements

The Plymouth settlers had bought land from the Indians about 10 miles (16 km) north of Huys de Hoop. The Indians called this spot Matianuck. The English first called it Dorchester and then Windsor. Holmes and his men erected a small house, then surrounded it with a stockade to keep out the Dutch and unfriendly Indians. Within two years, about 60 English settlers from Massachusetts Bay settled on land near the Windsor fort. The two communities in the Windsor area later merged.

stockade—a tall wooden fence built around a building or village for defense

In the meantime, the English were also busy about 5 miles (8 km) south of Huys de Hoop. A trader and explorer named John Oldham traveled by land from Massachusetts to Connecticut in August 1633. He had heard of Wahginnacut's offer to John Winthrop and decided to act on his own. The Wongunk gave Oldham and three companions food and furs. Oldham returned in 1634 with ten people and built a trading post and houses in what is now called Wethersfield.

PROFILE

John Oldham

John Oldham (c. 1600–1636) had arrived in Plymouth Colony from England in 1623. Unlike the Puritans who founded Plymouth, Oldham was more interested in making money than finding religious freedom. Within a few months of his arrival, he quarreled with the colony's leaders over how the colony was run, and they forced him out of Plymouth. He became a successful trader in Massachusetts before making his trip to Connecticut in 1633. After helping to found Wethersfield, Oldham spent time trading with Indians along Long Island Sound. In 1636, he was killed by Niantic Indians from Block Island, just off the shore of Connecticut in Long Island Sound. The relationship between the Niantic, an ally of the Pequot, and the English at the time was escalating toward armed conflict. Oldham's murder played a part in sparking the Pequot War of 1637, the bloodiest conflict between Connecticut settlers and the local tribes.

Land even farther south was also about to come under English settlement. In 1631, a group of English lords had received a grant of land at the mouth of the Connecticut River. John Winthrop, Jr., son of the Massachusetts governor, was chosen to lead a settlement there that was later called Saybrook. In the fall of 1635, Winthrop, Jr., sent Lion Gardiner, an English military engineer, to take control of the land and build a fort on the site. In 1636, a number of Puritans—the largest group yet of English colonists—were preparing to leave Massachusetts for a new home along the Connecticut River.

Puritan—a Protestant whose faith was based on the Bible rather than the teachings of church leaders

Fort Saybrook, built in 1636, was Connecticut's third-oldest settlement and its first military outpost.

CHAPTER TWO

The Puritans of Connecticut

PURITANS SETTLE IN THE NEW WORLD *and branch out from Massachusetts to settle Hartford. English troops battle the Pequot in Mystic, Connecticut.*

The Puritan faith developed in England during the 16th century, after King Henry VIII created a new church called the Anglican Church—or the Church of England. The new faith was called the Protestant religion because it protested various Roman Catholic practices.

Protestants believed that strictly following the teachings of the Bible was more important than doing good deeds or following what church leaders preached. These

OPPOSITE: Thomas Hooker (with walking stick) and his congregation rest during their journey from Massachusetts to Connecticut, where they will settle the town of Hartford.

people became known as Puritans. The Puritans also believed that only a small number of people, called the elect, were chosen by God to enter heaven. A Puritan had no way of knowing if he or she was one of the elect. Still, Puritans wanted to act as if they were chosen, which meant following all God's laws.

During the 1620s, King Charles I of England, an Anglican, began to make life difficult for the Puritans. He saw them as a threat to his rule, since they ignored laws of the Church of England. Charles began to limit the practice of Puritan religious services. Thomas Hooker, a popular Puritan minister, was one of the Puritan leaders who decided the time had come to leave England and make North America his new home. In 1631, Hooker said, *"God makes account that New England shall be a refuge . . . a rock and a shelter for his righteous ones to run unto; and those that were [upset] to see the ungodly lives of the people in this wicked land shall there be safe."*

The Separatists

The Separatists made up one group of English Puritans. They did not believe that the Anglican Church would ever change enough to truly reflect their religious beliefs. The Separatists thought they had to completely separate from the Anglican Church in order to worship as they chose. In 1620, a group of Separatists, along with some people who did not accept their Separatist views, sailed to New England on the *Mayflower*. Together, they are now known as the Pilgrims of Plymouth Colony. Although some Plymouth residents founded Windsor in 1633, they lost influence in Connecticut to the Puritans of Massachusetts Bay.

charter—a legal document that spells out a person's or group's rights and duties

In 1629, a trading company called the Massachusetts Bay Company obtained a charter from the king. The charter gave the company leaders control of land in Massachusetts. The charter also let the company leaders set up their own government, giving the Crown less control than it would have in most other English colonies in North America. Four hundred mostly Puritan settlers, including Thomas Hooker, departed for North America to create a society whose government would reflect their Puritan beliefs. John Winthrop was chosen governor of the new colony, which was named Massachusetts Bay.

One important belief of the Massachusetts Bay Puritans was the need for local citizens to control their own lives. The Massachusetts Bay Puritans were Congregationalists. They believed that each local church, or congregation, had the power to choose its ministers and run its own affairs. In both religious and political matters, the Congregationalists thought people should reach decisions together. This was a form of democracy, though only male members of the local church had the right to vote.

Heading to Hartford

John Cotton was a minister who arrived in Massachusetts Bay in 1633. Settling in Boston, he quickly became the chief minister of the colony. Thomas Hooker, serving as the pastor in Newtown (present-day Cambridge, Massachusetts), disagreed with some of Cotton's teachings. Cotton believed that people could do nothing to earn God's grace, while Hooker said believers could win God's favor through their actions. Hooker was also more willing to let new members join a congregation. He believed people should have greater power over their elected officials, called magistrates, than Massachusetts Bay allowed. Hooker also argued that all men, not just landholders and clergy, should have the right to vote.

In 1634, Hooker and some other leaders in Newtown asked for permission to leave Massachusetts Bay and start a new community. Governor John Winthrop feared that the move would weaken Massachusetts Bay and "*expose [the Newtown residents] to evident peril both from the Dutch [in New Netherland] . . . and from the Indians.*" Despite these arguments, in July 1635, six men from Newtown traveled to meet with the Sukiaug Indians near the Dutch fort of Huys de Hoop. The Puritans found that the Indians were eager to have them as neighbors, and Samuel Stone, Hooker's religious assistant, bought land from them. That October, John Winthrop noted, "*About 60 men, women, and little children went by land toward Connecticut with their cows, horses, and swine, and after a tedious and difficult journey arrived safe there.*" In the spring of 1636, Hooker and Stone led a hundred more people from Newtown to their new home. When they arrived, they saw a stockade surrounding a little village dotted

dugout—a simple shelter carved out of the side of a hill

with dugouts. Soon the residents were adding simple wooden houses and a meetinghouse, where they held religious services and ran the government of the settlement. They called their settlement Hartford, named for Stone's hometown of Hertford, England.

Hartford, Windsor, and Wethersfield were soon known as the river towns, and together they were called the River Colony. The river towns became the heart of the region of Connecticut. But first, the settlers had to make a deal with Massachusetts Bay officials. Technically, the Puritans of Connecticut had no legal right to the land they claimed. The English lords who controlled Saybrook had the only legal right to govern in Connecticut. However, John Winthrop, Sr., convinced Massachusetts officials to let the Connecticut Puritans set up their own government. It was called the General Court. The court's magistrates would make laws, hear legal cases, and have the power to declare war. The settlers would also recognize John Winthrop, Jr,. as their governor for one year.

The First Church of Hartford, erected by Thomas Hooker in 1638

After that first year, the magistrates would work with representatives from the river towns to run the General Court.

The Pequot War

The Connecticut General Court faced its first major crisis in 1637. The year before, Niantic Indians from Block Island had killed John Oldham. These Indians and the Pequot were allies, and fears arose that the Pequot were planning a war against the English. Massachusetts Bay responded first, sending a force of 90 men to Block Island. The soldiers burned the Niantic's wigwams and crops before heading to the main Pequot village on the mainland, near what is now Mystic, Connecticut. There the English once again destroyed Indian crops and homes.

The Massachusetts forces soon returned home, leaving Connecticut settlers near Saybrook open to attack. The Pequot had warned the settlers, *"We are Pequots . . . and can kill [Englishmen] as mosquitoes, and we will go to Connecticut and kill men, women, and children."* In April 1637, a Pequot force of about 200 raided Wethersfield, killing several men and kidnapping two young girls. On May 1, the General Court ordered that *"there shall be an offensive war against the Pequot."* The River Colony sent 90 men to help Saybrook's Lion Gardiner defend his town. Aiding the settlers were the Mohegan and their sachem, Uncas. The Narragansett of Rhode Island also sent help.

PROFILE

Uncas

Uncas (c. 1588–c. 1683) was descended from a long line of sachems with ties to the Pequot, Mohegan, and other Algonquian tribes. He married the daughter of a Pequot sachem, creating stronger ties between the two peoples. But Uncas disliked the Pequot's efforts to control the Indian trade with the Europeans, so he broke with the Pequot and turned to the English. As trouble began in 1636 between the English and the Indians, he encouraged the settlers of New England to attack the Pequot. Uncas knew a Pequot defeat would strengthen the Mohegan. He was right.

In 1643, after the Pequot War, Uncas (pictured here) defeated the Narragansett, led by Sachem Miantonomah. The Mohegan became the dominant tribe in eastern Connecticut for several decades. But Uncas could not stop the flow of settlers into the colony, and he was forced to sell off more and more of the Mohegan's lands.

A 19th-century wood engraving illustrates the battle between Pequot and English colonists, commanded by Captain John Mason, at the Indian fort near Stonington, Connecticut. Few Pequot survived the conflict.

On the morning of May 26, the English and their allies attacked a Pequot village. Within an hour, the battle was over, and the English suffered only a few casualties. The Pequot who survived the battle were forced to live in Mohegan and Narragansett villages, and the Mohegan became the dominant tribe of eastern

casualty—a soldier who is killed, wounded, or captured during a battle

Connecticut. Colonist John Mason gave this description of the attack on the Pequot village:

> *When [the fire] was thoroughly kindled the Indians ran as men most dreadfully amazed. And indeed such a dreadful terror did the Almighty let fall upon their spirits that they would fly from us and run into the very flames, where many of them perished. . . . The fire . . . did swiftly over-run the fort, to the extreme amazement of the enemy, and great rejoicing of our selves.*

A New Colony

During the time of the Pequot War, a new group of Puritan settlers reached Boston. Led by John Davenport, these colonists wanted to settle near a good harbor so they could easily trade with London, the capital of England. They also wanted to avoid the control of the Massachusetts Bay Puritans. Davenport heard reports of a bay in Connecticut west of Saybrook, so in March 1638, he sailed for a spot the Indians called *Quinnipiac.* The settlers later renamed it New Haven. They bought land from the local Algonquian tribes, making one purchase with *"eleven coats made of [coarse wool] cloth and one coat for [the chief's son] made of English cloth, made up after the English manner."* The New Haven settlers created a covenant, the foundation for all Puritan governments in

covenant—a formal agreement or contract

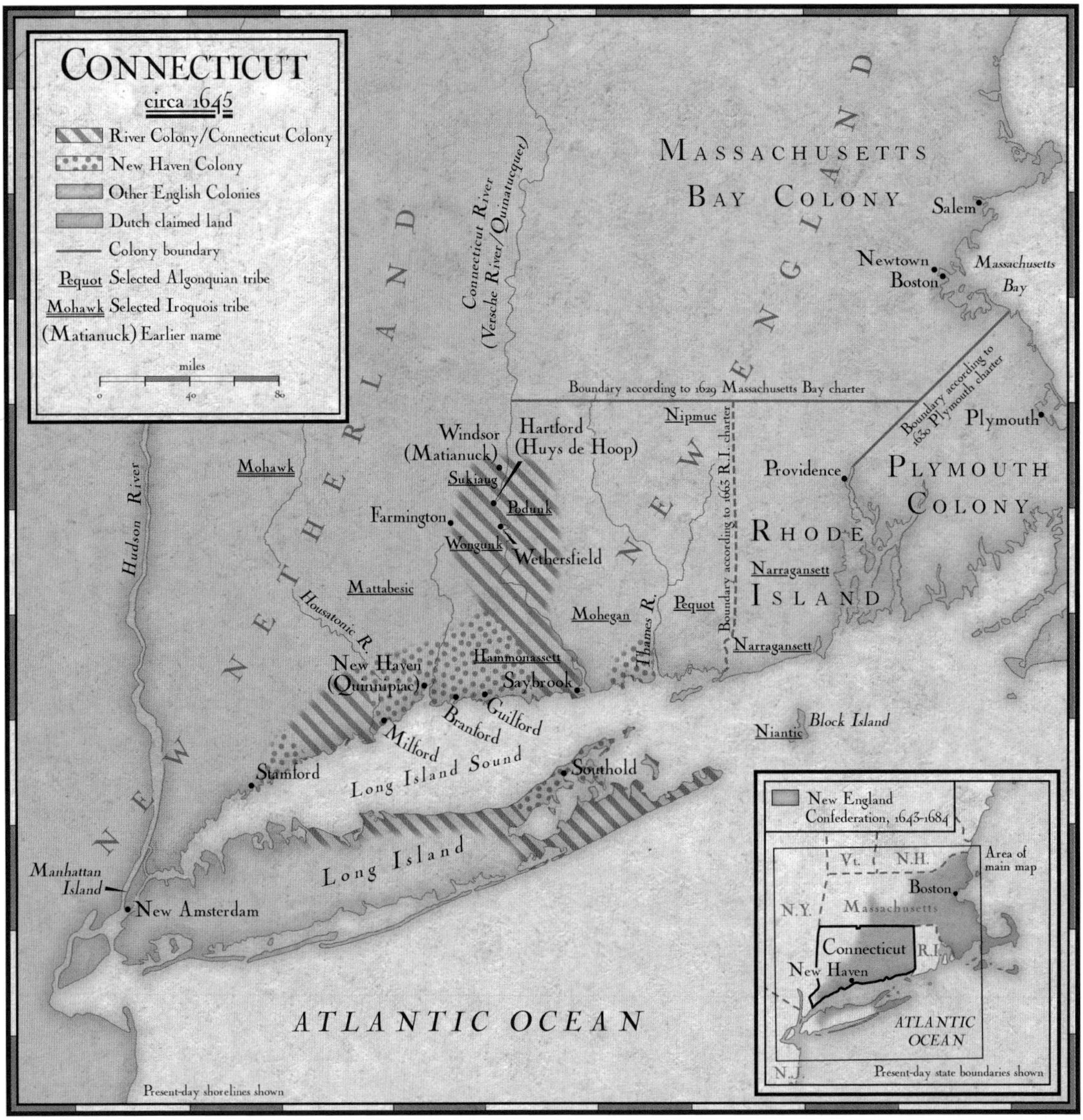

Ignoring Dutch claims to the land, English Puritans from Plymouth and Massachusetts Bay settled along the Connecticut River and Long Island Sound on lands they purchased from Native American peoples. By 1645, the settlements of Windsor, Wethersfield, and Hartford had united to form River Colony, which became known as Connecticut. New Haven was separate, with its own government. Concerns about attacks by Indians and the Dutch led both colonies to become part of the New England Confederation (see inset map) in 1643.

freeman—a landowner with voting rights

New England. The freemen joined together to create a government that would serve the interests of all residents in the colony.

At about the same time, Thomas Hooker was considering what kind of government the River Colony should have. In a sermon delivered in 1638, Hooker asserted his strong political belief that *"the foundation of authority is laid, firstly, in the free consent of the people."* When people voted or made government decisions, they should follow *"the blessed will and law of God."*

Hooker's sermon came as leaders of the River Colony were writing the Fundamental Orders. Completed in 1639, this document spelled out the basic workings of the government. In each town, freemen would elect men to represent them at the General Court. Unlike in Massachusetts, voters did not have to belong to a Congregational Church, although most were members. The General Court would meet to pass laws and choose officials, such as the governor, lieutenant governor, secretary, and treasurer. In the Fundamental Orders, the three river towns also stated their desire to *"maintain and preserve the liberty and purity of the gospel of our lord Jesus."*

CHAPTER THREE

Daily Life in the First Settlements

CONNECTICUT FARMERS CLEAR LAND *and plant crops including tobacco. Shipbuilding becomes a profitable industry as New Haven gains importance as a port.*

The rich farmland of the Connecticut River Valley had drawn the Puritans to Connecticut, and the settlers soon began preparing the fields for crops. Along the river, meadowlands were easily plowed. Farther from the river, farmers had to clear trees and remove rocks from the soil.

OPPOSITE: The hard work of harvesting crops was shared by the whole family, as seen in this engraving of a Connecticut farm family. The youngest child in the family is suspended in a sling above his mother while she toils cutting wheat.

Farm Life

Indians had taught the English to plant several seeds of corn together and use fish heads to fertilize the soil. Pumpkins or squash were also planted with the corn, and in between the corn and squash grew beans that also helped fertilize the earth. Because corn was so plentiful—and coins were in short supply—the General Court allowed residents to use it as money. Farmers also planted wheat, rye, and vegetables that they had raised in England.

Almost everyone in Connecticut farmed to feed their families, adding to their diets by hunting and fishing. Some farmers were able to raise more food than they needed and sold it in markets, increasing the family's wealth. Soon after the river towns were established, the General Court called for a weekly market in Hartford. The market was for

"all manner of [goods] that shall be brought in, and for cattle, or any merchandise whatsoever."

merchandise—goods sold in a store or market

The first Connecticut farmers sometimes worked the land as a group, even though each family also owned its own plots. Residents also shared the Commons, a central pasture where cattle, pigs, oxen, and other animals grazed. Town leaders divided individual farming plots so that families received a mix of the best and worst land. This division, however, meant that one farmer's land might be spread out over a wide area. As farms expanded, residents on the edges of a town often asked town officials for permission to start their own congregation.

One danger farmers outside of town faced was wolves. In 1699, Samuel Smith wrote down his memories of his boyhood in Wethersfield. He said wolves were *"the great terror of our lives....The noise of their howling was enough to curdle the blood of the [strongest]."* Local governments offered money to hunters to kill the dangerous animals, which killed livestock.

A LEAFY CROP

ALTHOUGH CONNECTICUT never had the large tobacco plantations cultivated in the southern colonies of Virginia and Maryland, some tobacco was grown in the colony. Around 1640, Windsor farmers began raising the same kind that the local Indians grew. English smokers found this tobacco to taste too harsh, so Connecticut farmers switched to a type of tobacco raised in English colonies in the West Indies. This type of plant, called wrap tobacco, is still grown in Connecticut today.

OTHER PROFESSIONS

Although most people farmed, some Connecticut residents earned their living by other skills. Blacksmiths, woodworkers, brickmakers, or tailors were usually found in every town, as was a miller, who turned corn or wheat into grain. Each town also had an innkeeper, who rented beds to visitors and served food and drink. One of Windsor's first residents was a doctor, Bray Rossiter, who had studied medicine in Europe. In 1640, New Haven officials gave Peter Brown a license to "*to bake bread to sell so long as he gives no offenset.*"

The fur trade had attracted the Dutch to Connecticut, and the English traded for furs as well. Driven by European fashions, the industry grew, spurring greater exploration and expansion of Connecticut and the New World. The Connecticut towns of Windsor and Hartford had been built around a trading post, and the first settlers of New Haven built a post to obtain beaver skins from the Indians. Starting in the 1640s, Connecticut residents began using lumber from the colony's abundant forests to build ships, so their crops and other goods could be traded in New Amsterdam (New York City) and Boston. Those goods included animal hides, livestock, and barrel staves. Farmers and craftsmen sold their goods to local merchants, who transported them to the large towns within Connecticut, such as New Haven, which was closer to the Atlantic. The merchants then traded the goods for items such as sugar, molasses, glassware, pewter, spices, and guns. Most of this merchandise arrived in New Amsterdam and Boston from overseas. Soon, transport industries developed to take goods north and south of these points. In 1650, to make trade and travel as easy as possible, the General Court required men to work two days every year to keep the roads in good shape. The government also forced some towns to build bridges over rivers.

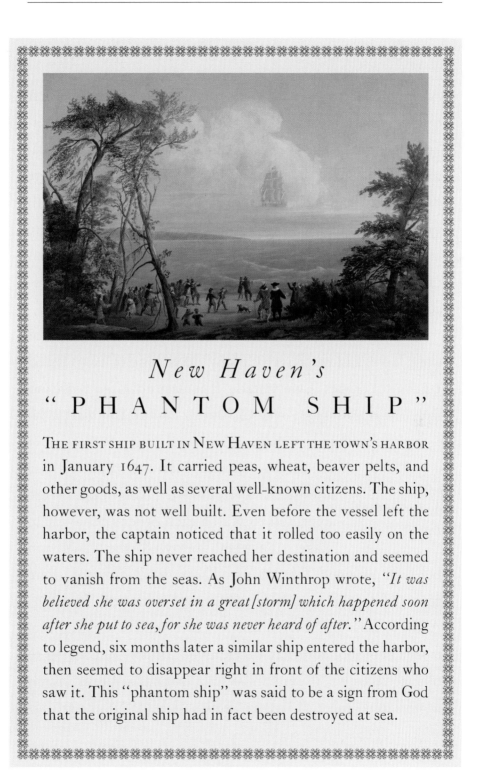

New Haven's "PHANTOM SHIP"

THE FIRST SHIP BUILT IN NEW HAVEN LEFT THE TOWN'S HARBOR in January 1647. It carried peas, wheat, beaver pelts, and other goods, as well as several well-known citizens. The ship, however, was not well built. Even before the vessel left the harbor, the captain noticed that it rolled too easily on the waters. The ship never reached her destination and seemed to vanish from the seas. As John Winthrop wrote, "*It was believed she was overset in a great [storm] which happened soon after she put to sea, for she was never heard of after.*" According to legend, six months later a similar ship entered the harbor, then seemed to disappear right in front of the citizens who saw it. This "phantom ship" was said to be a sign from God that the original ship had in fact been destroyed at sea.

Religion in Daily Life

As each new town was founded in Connecticut, the first task was building a meetinghouse and selecting a minister. Services were held twice on Sunday and on special occasions, such as days of thanksgiving. In homes, fathers were expected to lead their families in prayer and teach their children Puritan beliefs. Taxes to support the local church were at first voluntary, but in 1644, the General Court ruled that taxpayers—all landowners and males over the age of 16—could be forced to pay their fair share for the church.

Puritans in Connecticut used the Bible as a basis for their laws, and the River Colony's law code of 1650 listed 14 capital crimes. One stated, "*If any man after legal conviction shall have or worship any other God but the Lord God, he shall be put to death.*" Another law made it a capital crime to "*conspire or attempt any invasion, insurrection, or rebellion against the [government].*" Neighbors were expected to watch each other's behavior to make sure they followed the laws and behaved as good Christians. Those who did not were reported to the local magistrates and punished. In 1643, Andrew Low of New Haven was arrested for stealing rum from a neighbor and then breaking out of jail. According to official records, "*it was [then] ordered that he shall be as severely whipped as the rule will bare, and work with his father as a prisoner with a lock upon his leg so that he may not escape.*"

capital crime—referring to a crime that is punishable by death

WITCHCRAFT

During times of crisis, some Puritans grew suspicious of neighbors who didn't fit in or who caused trouble. The devil was often blamed for the neighbors' actions, and some were labeled "witches." The Salem, Massachusetts, witch trials of 1692 are well known today, but Connecticut had its own "witch hunts." The first Connecticut witch hunt took place in Hartford between 1661 and 1663. During this period, eight-year old Elizabeth Kelley was heard to cry out, "*Help me, help me, [the witch] is upon me* . . . ." Kelley died, and Dr. Bray Rossiter examined her body. He declared that witchcraft had caused her death.

During the first witch hunt, about eight people were accused of using witchcraft to harm others. Three women were found guilty of being witches and were killed. Several other people accused of witchcraft fled the colony rather than face trial. The second notable witch hunt in Connecticut took place in 1692 near Stamford. News of the Salem witches had reached the area, causing some local residents there to think they had their own witches. Seven women were accused, including Elizabeth Clauson. At her trial, dozens of neighbors defended her. The statement they signed said, "*. . . we have not known her to be of a contentious frame . . . but hath been civil and orderly* . . . . " Clauson and the other accused women were finally released. The last witch trial in Connecticut—and perhaps all of America—took place in 1697. Once again, the accused witches were found innocent.

Family Life

Connecticut Puritans believed that God had created a certain order among people. A man was the head of a family, and his wife and children were expected to obey him. He was expected to love his family and provide the best he could for them in spiritual and practical matters.

When a woman married, any property she owned became her husband's. She lost her legal right to sue someone in court or sign a contract. Widows and single adult women, however, had those legal rights because they had to provide for themselves. No women, however, could vote or serve in the government.

The first families of Connecticut lived in simple wooden houses, with one or two rooms on each of two floors. A few families lived in bigger houses that had one floor about 60 feet (18 m) long and 15 feet (5 m) wide. These copied a style of housing in England that dated back to the 9th century. In 2000, archaeologists working in Andover discovered remains of one of these "long houses"—the first ever found in Connecticut.

archaeologist—a scientist who studies the past by uncovering items people used in their daily lives

In and around the home, everyone except the youngest children was expected to work. Husbands ran the farm or the family business, while their wives cooked, cleaned, made clothing, and raised the children. Daughters helped with chores such as making butter, growing vegetables, and spinning wool into yarn. Sons helped their fathers in the fields and chopped wood for the fireplace. They also learned whatever other skills their fathers had, such as milling or carpentry.

EDUCATING AND RAISING THE YOUNG

By law, Connecticut parents were expected to teach their children the Christian faith and give them *"so much learning as may enable them perfectly to read the English tongue, and knowledge of the capital laws."* Large towns, with more than 100 families, were expected to build a grammar school, but for most of the 17th century, few Connecticut towns had the money to hire teachers and build schools so parents taught their children to read.

Parents were required to teach their children a skill and train them *"in some honest, lawful calling, labor, or employment, either in husbandry or some other trade profitable for themselves and [the colony]."* If parents failed in this duty, the government could take the children from their homes and make them apprentices. Apprentices were children who lived with a skilled person, such as a blacksmith or printer. They helped their masters do their daily work, and the masters were required to teach the apprentices how to read as well as the skills of their trade.

husbandry—farming and raising animals

CHAPTER FOUR

Creating a United Colony

A new English king declares all of the New England colonies under his control. The Glorious Revolution in England restores self-rule to Connecticut.

Local control was essential to the Connecticut Puritans, yet at times they saw the importance of working with others who shared their values, especially in matters of defense. Although the Pequot War of 1637 ended that tribe's danger for the colonists, the Narragansett Indians were still large in number. Also, the Dutch still claimed Connecticut as part of New Netherland.

OPPOSITE: This hand-colored woodcut shows English and Dutch farmers fighting over land in colonial Connecticut. Throughout the 1640s, the Dutch tried desperately to hold onto their lands and control of trade with the Pequot. But an English alliance with the Mohegan and Narragansett forced the Pequot off their land and killed any remaining members of the tribe, thus ending Dutch influence in the region.

Worried that their land and lives were in danger, officials in the river towns and New Haven talked with officials from Massachusetts Bay. In April 1643, the New Haven General Court sent commissioners from the colony to Massachusetts to discuss forming *"a general combination for all the plantations in New England . . . for the exalting of Christ's ends and advancing the public good in all the plantations."* Later that year, New Haven and the River Colony joined with Massachusetts Bay and Plymouth to form the United Colonies of New England, also called the New England Confederation. The confederation would coordinate defense—each of the four groups committing troops and money toward protection against the Dutch and Native Americans—and settle boundary disputes.

commissioner—a government official

This image of a rural area within the growing New Haven colony in 1637 shows a Dutch settler in front of his cabin along a waterway.

More Growth

By the time the New England Confederation was founded, more Puritans had settled in the River Colony and New Haven, which continued to operate with a separate government. To an extent, New Haven competed with the River Colony for settlers and trade. Gradually, new towns arose. In 1640, settlers from the River Colony moved westward and founded Farmington, and in 1647 the colony took control of a settlement at the mouth of the Thames River. The town was later named New London. By this time, Saybrook had also joined the River Colony, which was now known as Connecticut.

In New Haven, settlers spread out to found five new towns: Milford, Guilford, Branford, Stamford, and Southold, which was on Long Island. At first, the towns were independent, but in 1643 they came under the legal control of New Haven. That year, New Haven created its own governing document, which said that only members of the local Congregationalist churches could serve in the government.

A "Fair Harbor"

IN 1646, JOHN WINTHROP, JR., founded the settlement of Nameaug. Over the next dozen years the town was known by several names, including Pequot and Fair Harbor. That last name reflected what the River Colony lawmakers called the town's "*excellent harbor . . . a fit and convenient place for future trade.*" In 1648, lawmakers decided on the name New London. New London grew into an important city, thanks to its harbor, the deepest in the colony. In 1680, Connecticut leaders boasted that "*a ship of 500 tons [454 metric tons] may go up to the town, and come so near the shore that they may toss a biscuit ashore.*"

The Need for a Charter

During most of the 1640s and 1650s, Puritans battled Catholic supporters of King Charles I for control in England. In 1648, England's Puritans and their allies rejected Charles's authority to rule and, the next year, beheaded him. Another decade of civil war followed. In 1660, Parliament asked Charles's son to rule as King Charles II to restore peace and order.

The people of the River Colony realized that Charles II would probably pay more attention to England's American colonies than the previous government had. Charles, an Anglican, counted on his colonies for income, and he wanted to increase his influence over them. The founders of Massachusetts Bay had a charter that outlined their freedom to rule themselves largely as they chose. But the River Colony did not have the same legal guarantee of its independence. In 1661, the colony sent John Winthrop, Jr., now its governor, to secure a charter from Charles II.

New Haven was also worried about its political future. Many thought New Haven should work with the river towns to get one charter that would allow two separate governments in Connecticut. John Davenport, who had helped found New Haven, opposed this idea. The influence of the Congregational Church was weaker in the River Colony than in New Haven. Davenport feared that one charter for the two colonies would force New Haven to accept the River Colony's laws, which were less strict than New Haven's.

Reverend John Davenport is pictured in a late 17th-century engraving by artist Amos Doolittle.

Winthrop reached London in September 1661. New Haven officials had asked him to see about getting a separate charter for their colony, but Winthrop was more interested in protecting the rights of the River Colony. In that, he was hugely successful. In 1662, Charles gave him a charter that formally established the Connecticut Colony and allowed it to rule itself as it had since the Fundamental Orders of 1639. Connecticut residents would have more freedom than almost any other English colonists. The charter said, "*That for the better ordering and managing of the affairs and business of the said company . . . one governor, one deputy governor and twelve assistants to be from time to time constituted, elected and chosen out of the freemen of the said company.*" The General Court became known as the General Assembly and was composed of two houses. The governor's assistants formed one house, while elected representatives sent by the towns formed the other. The charter also set the colony's boundaries, giving it parts of land claimed by both Rhode Island and New Haven. In a generous mood, the king added that Connecticut's western boundary stretched to the "South Seas"—what is now called the Pacific Ocean.

PROFILE

John Winthrop, Jr.

Like his father, John Winthrop, Jr., (1606–1676) was a Puritan lawyer who chose to settle in New England. The younger Winthrop played a part in the founding of several Connecticut towns, but winning the 1662 charter for the colony was probably his greatest accomplishment. Although he served as governor of Connecticut for 18 years, he was much more than a politician. He was also a merchant, a scientist, and a doctor. Winthrop used an early telescope to find Jupiter's fifth moon, and he was elected a member of the Royal Society, a scientific group based in London. His son Fitz-John Winthrop also served as a governor of colonial Connecticut from 1698–1707.

Colonial Disagreements

Connecticut residents cheered Winthrop's success, but New Haven's leaders were angry. They had lost control of land they claimed, and they refused Connecticut's offer to become part of that colony. By the end of 1664, however, the towns outside New Haven agreed to become part of Connecticut, and the next year New Haven joined as well. A few of the New Haven Puritans who still opposed the new arrangement left the colony and founded a settlement in what is now New Jersey.

Connecticut's charter also led to conflicts with its neighbors. In 1664, England challenged the Dutch in New Netherland and took control of that colony, renaming it New York. The new colony was ruled by James, the brother of Charles II. The king declared that his brother's new lands included land claimed by New York on the western edge of the Connecticut River. Luckily for Connecticut, New York agreed to give up some of these lands. Still, it took more than half a century for the two colonies to officially establish their shared border.

The Last Indian War

The disagreements among the New England colonies were heated but never led to armed conflict. Connecticut had enjoyed a long period of peace after the Pequot War of 1637.

Preparing for the Worst

In October 1675, the Connecticut General Court took steps to control the Indians of Hartford. The lawmakers ordered

. . . that the constable of Hartford be appointed to take account of the Indian men, women and children . . . and give order that part of the watch keep constantly their eye upon them . . . that they see none do them wrong in word or action . . . and give them strict order that none be abroad after sunset, and none be absent but by [permission] or some English with them.

In 1675, however, fighting in Massachusetts between the settlers and the Wampanoag sparked a larger conflict called King Philip's War. Connecticut residents feared that the war would spread to their colony. On the whole, however, the Connecticut Indians remained friendly, and the only sign of war in the colony was the burning of most of Simsbury by Native Americans in March 1676.

Connecticut did send its soldiers to help the other New England colonies. In December 1675, several hundred troops took part in an attack on the Narragansett, destroying their main village. Connecticut soldiers also helped track down the Indians who escaped. King Philip's War lasted until the summer of 1676, after which the Indians of southern New England never again challenged the English colonists.

At a meeting between Captain Thomas Bull, the commanding officer at Fort Saybrook, and Sir Edmund Andros, governor of New York, at the mouth of the Connecticut River, Bull (left) orders Andros to cease reading his claims to the area and return to New York immediately.

Struggle With the Crown

The Indian threat was gone in Connecticut, but residents faced another worry. The royal governor of New York, Sir Edmund Andros, believed his authority extended east to the Connecticut River. In the summer of 1675, he traveled there to make his presence known to Connecticut residents. Upon his arrival, he was met at the mouth of the river by Captain Thomas Bull and his troops stationed at Fort Saybrook. When Andros attempted to read the royal order specifying his areas of control, Captain Bull ordered him to stop and immediately return to New York. Faced with a

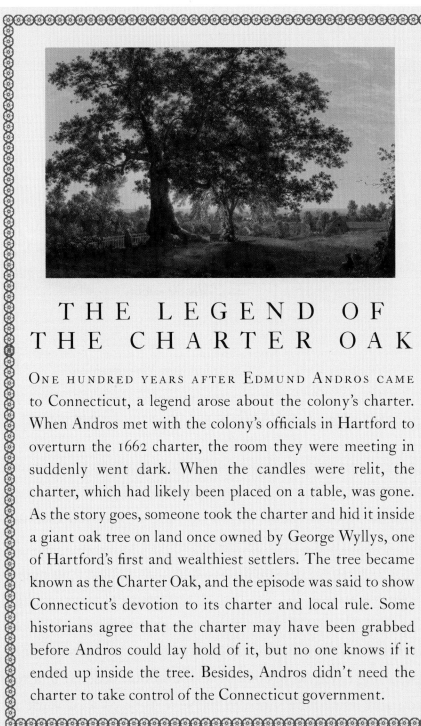

THE LEGEND OF THE CHARTER OAK

One hundred years after Edmund Andros came to Connecticut, a legend arose about the colony's charter. When Andros met with the colony's officials in Hartford to overturn the 1662 charter, the room they were meeting in suddenly went dark. When the candles were relit, the charter, which had likely been placed on a table, was gone. As the story goes, someone took the charter and hid it inside a giant oak tree on land once owned by George Wyllys, one of Hartford's first and wealthiest settlers. The tree became known as the Charter Oak, and the episode was said to show Connecticut's devotion to its charter and local rule. Some historians agree that the charter may have been grabbed before Andros could lay hold of it, but no one knows if it ended up inside the tree. Besides, Andros didn't need the charter to take control of the Connecticut government.

military show of force, Andros left, angry and humiliated. It would be more than a dozen years before he returned to Connecticut.

In 1686, English officials accused the colony of breaking English laws, including denying the freedom of worship to people who were not Congregationalists. James, the Roman Catholic brother of Charles II, was now king, and he ordered that all of New England should come under his direct control. He named Edmund Andros the governor of the newly named Dominion of New England. The dominion also included New York and New Jersey.

In October 1687, Andros arrived in the capital town of Hartford to assert his authority over Connecticut. Local officials later wrote, "*The good people of the colony, though they were under a great sense of the injuries they sustained . . . yet chose rather to be silent and patient than to oppose.*"

A revolt in England, however, soon ended Andros's rule. This event was known as the Glorious Revolution because the English reformed their government without spilling a drop of blood. Massachusetts residents took advantage of the change in English government to arrest Andros, who was living in Boston. With Andros gone, Connecticut soon went back to its old government based on the 1662 charter.

Servants and Slaves

COLONIAL RESIDENTS OF *Connecticut share their lives with indentured servants, African slaves, and Native Americans, all who contribute to the colony's growth and prosperity.*

The first settlers of Connecticut had plenty of land and relied on servants and slaves to help raise their crops, take care of their children, and run their businesses. In general, the small size of Connecticut farms kept the number of slaves and servants low, compared to the colonies farther south, such as Maryland and Virginia. In a report to England in 1680, Connecticut officials said, "*There are but few servants among us, and less slaves, not above 30.*"

OPPOSITE: Slave traders bargain with tribal leaders along the coast of Africa. Two slaves lie on the ground while one has his teeth checked before a prospective sale.

Servants, Bound and Free

In the early years of the River Colony and New Haven, most servants signed a contract called an indenture, so they were known as indentured—or bound—servants. By agreeing to work for a master without pay for a number of years, usually seven, they paid for their voyage to America. A master would supply their servant with food, clothing, and a place to live. Some young servants agreed to work until they reached 21. People already in Connecticut were sometimes forced to become servants if they had a debt they could not pay. Others were bound if they committed a crime and could not make restitution to their victim. Some Indians were also taken on as servants. Indian women helped colonial families raise their children, while Indian children often worked in the colonists' fields until their debts were repaid. Later in the 17th century and into the 18th century, Africans were also used as indentured servants.

restitution—payment made to offset a loss

Early Connecticut laws outlined what servants could not do. For example, *"no servant, either man or [woman], shall either give, sell, or truck any commodity whatsoever, without license from their master . . . under pain of fine or corporal [physical] punishment."* Servants were expected to work the full day—except Sunday—though masters had to allow them *"convenient time for food and rest."* Young servants who disobeyed their masters or otherwise caused trouble were subjected to *"hard labor and severe punishment.*" By the 18th century, almost all bound servants in Connecticut were Indians or Africans. Whites, if they were servants, were free, which meant they did not sign an indenture, and they received pay for their work. Women were most likely to work as servants in the home. Men commonly did farm work.

Indian Slavery in Connecticut

The English, like many peoples of the 17th century, enslaved the enemies they considered heathens after defeating them in battle. Christians of the time, including the Puritans, accepted slavery since it was allowed in the Bible. Since the slaves were not Christians, the slave owners considered them inferior. These slaves were different from bound servants. They were considered property and as such, owned for life by a master.

heathens—people who do not acknowledge the God of the Bible; uncivilized

The first large group of slaves in Connecticut was made up of Pequot, mostly women and children. They were enslaved after the Pequot War of 1637. John Mason wrote that he and his men took about "*one hundred eighty [captives]; whom we divided, intending to keep them as servants.*" Mason used the word "servants," but he meant slaves. Over time, Narragansett, Nipmuc, and Wampanoag joined the Pequot as slaves in Connecticut, as did Indians from the West Indies.

Like indentured Indian servants, Indian slaves helped raise settlers' children and grow their crops. Some masters freed their slaves when they were old and no longer useful. Still, records from New London in the late 17th century show that one 60-year-old Indian woman was still serving as a slave. In general, the colonists found that male Indian slaves were not the best source of labor. They resisted doing farmwork, since Indian men were raised to be hunters, so the women and children did most of the farm work.

A page from the logbook of Connecticut-born Samuel Gould, first mate aboard a slave ship from 1775 to 1778, gives information about the day's weather, the health of various slaves on board, and the course, winds, and distance the ship has traveled.

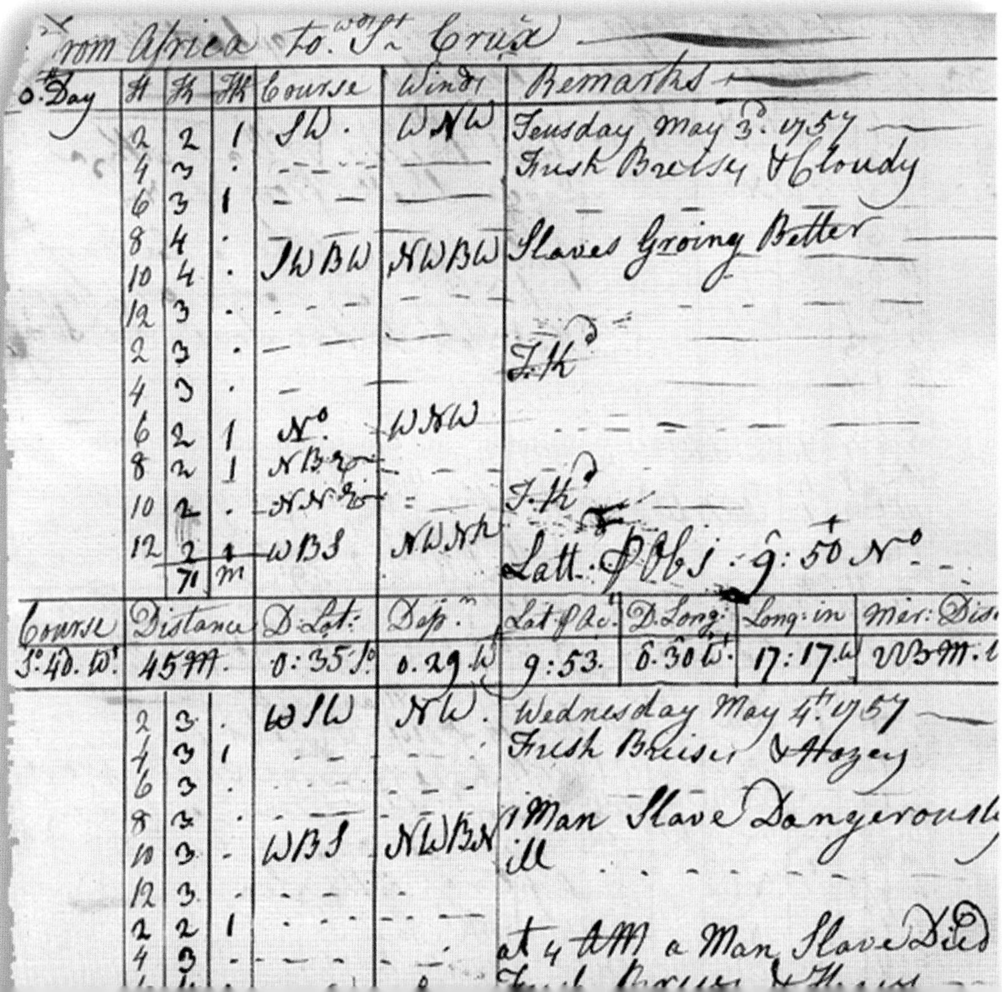

In the early 1700s, Indian slaves of both sexes became less common. Indentured and enslaved Indians usually lived near free Indians. Some of the free Indians lived in English towns, while others lived on tribal lands outside the settlers' towns. The presence of free Indians meant that Indian slaves who ran away had a good chance of finding refuge with local tribes. To limit escapes, Connecticut lawmakers in 1676 rewarded free Indians who turned in runaways, promising them two yards of cloth. But free Indians who hid fugitives, the law said, "*shall be liable to pay forty shillings for every such offense or suffer one month's imprisonment.*" Many Connecticut masters came to prefer African slaves, since runaways could not find refuge as easily as Indians.

shilling—an English coin used in colonial times that would be worth about $12 today

African Slavery in Connecticut

The first African slaves in Connecticut probably came with the Dutch. Gysbert Opdyck of Huys de Hoop was said to have a slave. By 1639, some Africans came to the Hartford area with white masters who had lived in Massachusetts. In New Haven, both of that colony's major founders, John Davenport and Theophilus Eaton, owned slaves. Like Indians, these Africans were often called servants, but most were actually slaves, bound for life to a master. These slaves were just a few of the estimated 12 million Africans forced out of their homeland and enslaved from 1450 to 1850, the main years of the Atlantic slave trade. The largest numbers went to South America and the islands of the Caribbean. Through the 17th century, small numbers of African slaves were bought in the West Indies and brought to Connecticut. Their numbers rose in the 18th century, especially after 1749, as more settlers could afford to buy slaves. Masters tended to be wealthy merchants and farmers or professionals such as lawyers, ministers, and government officials who used slaves to work in their homes. Most masters owned only one or a few slaves. By 1774, the thriving seaport of New London had more than 500 blacks, mostly slaves, more than any other town in the colony.

Slave Life

As the number of Africans in the colony grew, Connecticut officials passed laws limiting their freedoms. After 1690, slaves, both African and Indian, could not go out beyond town limits without written permission from their masters or local magistrates. In the 18th century, Connecticut passed even more laws restricting the movement of blacks, both slave and free. A 1708 law noted that African and mulatto slaves were *"often quarreling with white people to the great disturbance of the peace."* To stop such disputes, the law said *"that if any negro or mulatto servant or slave disturb the*

mulatto—of mixed Caucasian (white) and black ancestry

peace, or shall offer to strike any white person . . . [he] shall be punished by whipping . . . not exceeding thirty stripes for one offense."

Despite the laws restricting what slaves could do, not all were treated badly. And they enjoyed some legal rights. African slaves in Connecticut who worked on farms or in their master's home usually lived in their master's house. In 1704, when Sarah Kemble Knight, a shopkeeper and businesswoman in Massachusetts visited Connecticut, she found it odd that masters and slaves ate together. She also noted that one dispute between a master and a slave was brought to local officials. The officials, *"having heard the allegations of both parties, order[ed] the master to pay 40 shillings to [the slave], and acknowledge [the master's] fault."* In 1730, a law spelled out a slave's rights to file legal complaints and give evidence in court. The children of slaves were taught to read, and Africans were allowed to be baptized in Congregational churches. They attended the same churches as their masters, but sat in a separate section.

FUGITIVE SLAVES

SLAVES WHO RECEIVED HARSH treatment or simply wanted their freedom back sometimes ran away. Masters placed ads in the local papers seeking their return. One ad published in New London in 1759 described a slave *"named Nero, about 20 years old; a well looking fellow, of middling stature ... speaks broken English ...; he went away in irons, which it is likely he has got off.... Whoever shall take up said Negro and convey him to his said master shall have five dollars reward."*

Starting around 1750, a highlight for Connecticut's African slaves was Election Day. When their masters went to Hartford to select a governor, the slaves went with them for a celebration called 'Lection Day. With the approval of their masters, the slaves met to choose one slave to serve as their governor. Though this person had no legal power, he was usually a respected slave owned by a wealthy master. After the election, the slaves held a parade and a festival. The first recorded black governor was a slave called London, who was chosen in 1755. Over the decades, slaves held elections in other towns, such as New London, New Haven, and Norwich, to elect local governors. The governors handed out punishments to slaves who harmed other slaves and tried to help slaves settle disputes with whites.

Ways to Freedom

Not all Africans in Connecticut were slaves. As noted before, some were indentured servants. When their contracts ended, they were free to go out on their own. Some African slaves were freed by their masters. Some masters wrote in their wills that, upon their death, their slaves would be granted freedom. Also, many masters gave their slaves a chance to earn money working for other colonists. Slaves who saved this money could use it to buy their own freedom. Free African Americans could own property and work at any job they had the skills for.

PROFILE

Venture Smith

One of the most well-known free blacks in Connecticut was Venture Smith. Smith was born in Africa in 1729. At six, he was sold into slavery and eventually came to live in Connecticut. By the time he was 31, Smith had earned enough money to buy his freedom. He then bought his wife and children and eventually owned a 100-acre (41-ha) farm in East Haddam. In his 1798 autobiography, Smith described a scene with his master's wife, who was arguing with Smith's wife: "*my mistress turned the blows which she was repeating on my wife to me. She took down her horse whip, and while she was [satisfying] her fury with it, I reached out my great black hand, raised it up and received the blows of the whip on it which were designed for my head. Then I immediately committed the whip to the devouring fire.*"

Through the 18th century, however, laws in Connecticut increasingly restricted what freed slaves could do. A 1717 law said free blacks and mulattoes could not own land or live in Connecticut towns. This law, however, and others that tried to limit the actions of blacks were not always enforced. And in at least one case, white voters in Farmington chose a free black man to hold public office. Frank Freeman was elected to serve as the animal control officer.

CHAPTER SIX

New Challenges

Religious groups become *splintered as the Great Awakening comes to Connecticut. The Connecticut militia responds to Britain's call for troops to help fight in the French and Indian War.*

During the 1600s, France established a colony in North America called New France, centered in what is now Canada. In 1690, the French colonists and their Indian allies threatened the safety of New York and New England. The French wanted to control the fur trade around the Great Lakes and St. Lawrence River Valley. Their interests in the region sometimes clashed with England's desire to trade with the Indians and

OPPOSITE: George Whitefield, the most well-known preacher of the Great Awakening, preaches to a crowd in the middle of a field in Connecticut in the mid-1700s.

expand the English claim to the region. For several years, the French and Indians threatened the peace along the New England frontier in what the colonists called King William's War.

By 1701, after France and England signed a peace treaty, King William's War ended. In Connecticut, two major events took place that year. The General Assembly decided to make New Haven a second capital for the colony. Until then, the government had met in Hartford twice a year. From now on, one session would be held in New Haven and one in Hartford. New Haven and Hartford served as co-capitals of Connecticut through 1875, after which Hartford became the sole capital.

A woodcut of students gathered on the lawn of Yale College in New Haven, Connecticut, in 1784.

Also in 1701, Connecticut's first college received a charter from the government. It was called the Collegiate School, and there, the charter said, "*youth may be instructed in the arts and sciences [and] through the blessing of Almighty God may be fitted for public employment both in church and civil state.*" The Collegiate School was founded in Saybrook, but in 1718 it moved to New Haven, where it was renamed Yale College. Today it is known as Yale University, one of the top colleges in the United States.

The Great Awakening

By the 1730s, Connecticut was no longer a strictly Congregationalist colony. Puritan teachings still influenced the government, and all taxpayers had to support the local Congregational churches. But other Protestants had come to the colony, including members of the Society of Friends, also called Quakers; Baptists; and especially Anglicans, also called Episcopalians.

Another challenge to traditional Congregational ways came from a movement called the Great Awakening. It began in the American colonies during the 1720s and reached its peak in Connecticut during the 1740s. The movement influenced social and political thought throughout the colonies. During the Great Awakening, some ministers traveled from town to town to hold meetings called revivals. The ministers wanted people to denounce their sins and "awaken" to a new, deeper faith in Jesus Christ. Nathan Cole, a colonist who attended a revival in Middletown and later wrote a book about it, described the large audience as *"a steady stream of horses and their riders, . . . every horse seemed to go with all his might to carry his rider to hear the news from heaven for the saving of their souls."*

PROFILE

Jonathan Edwards

One of the American leaders of the Great Awakening was Jonathan Edwards (1703–1758). Born in East Windsor, Connecticut, Edwards was the son and grandson of Congregationalist ministers. He attended Yale, then began serving as the minister in Northampton, Massachusetts, in 1726. Edwards sometimes returned to Connecticut to give sermons. He gave his best-known sermon—perhaps the most famous American sermon of all time—while visiting Enfield, Connecticut, in 1741. Edwards called the talk "Sinners in the Hands of an Angry God." In it he warned, "*Your wickedness makes you . . . tend downward with great weight and pressure toward hell; and if God should let you go, you would immediately sink and swiftly descend and plunge into the bottomless gulf.*" Only by accepting Jesus Christ as their savior, Edwards preached, could the wicked avoid hell.

At first, most Congregationalists saw value in the Great Awakening. Deepening religious beliefs, they thought, was a good thing. But over time, a split arose. The people who accepted the ideas of the revival ministers were called New Lights. They argued with traditional Congregationalists, called Old Lights. Some Old Light ministers disliked that the revival ministers appealed to emotions rather than to reason. And some of the New Light speakers were not ministers at all. Joshua Hempstead, an Old Light from New London, heard one of these traveling preachers, James Davenport, great-grandson of John Davenport of New Haven. Hempstead wrote, "*It was difficult to distinguish between his praying and preaching for it was all mere confused medley. . . . I can't relate the inconsistance of it.*" Congregations sometimes split apart as New and Old Lights battled for control.

By challenging established churches and ministers, New Lights also threatened the political order of the day. In 1742, the General Assembly limited who could preach and where they could do it. Over time, however, the lawmakers gave more Protestants greater freedom to worship as they chose.

Foreign Wars

The battles over religion did not turn violent, but Connecticut residents were not strangers to actual conflict. The 1701 peace between France and England after King William's War did not end their clashes in North America.

Louisbourg

In 1743, France and Great Britain fought again, in a conflict called King George's War (1743–1748). The French had a massive fort called Louisbourg on Cape Breton Island, north of Novia Scotia. From there, French ships sailed from Louisbourg to capture New England merchant vessels.

In 1745, Massachusetts governor William Shirley proposed that New England forces unite to attack Louisbourg. The Connecticut General Assembly agreed, believing that New England *"can expect no safety until . . . Cape Breton and Canada can be subdued."* The capture of Louisbourg in June 1745 was the highlight of the war for the New Englanders and a major British military success. However, in the peace treaty that ended King George's War, Great Britain and France agreed to give back lands they had seized from each other, and Louisbourg returned to French control.

Over the next 60 years, they fought a series of wars, with each side relying on Indian allies. Connecticut was not as exposed to enemy attack as Massachusetts or northern New York. Still, its residents played a part in the wars.

In 1704, the French and their Indian allies carried out a deadly raid on Deerfield, Massachusetts, just 35 miles (56 km) north of the Connecticut border. The raid pushed leaders of Connecticut to prepare for war. The colony sent troops to fight in Massachusetts and sent scouts to the frontier to watch for enemy action.

The Deerfield raid was part of a larger war called Queen Anne's War (1702–1713). The war included battles in Europe. For Connecticut troops, the main activity of the war was helping British troops seize Port Royal, in Nova Scotia, a region of New France on the Atlantic Ocean.

Continuing Conflict With the French and Indians

The competition between France and Great Britain to control the fur trade sparked their last and biggest war in North America. In 1754, a young Virginia officer named George Washington fought French and Indian forces in the Ohio River Valley. These were the first battles of what Americans later called the French and Indian War (1754–1763). Other battles in the war were fought in the West Indies and Europe.

This painting illustrates the 1755 battle in which British General Edward Braddock and his men are ambushed and defeated by French and Indian troops as they attempt to take Fort Duquesne (now present-day Pittsburgh) from French control during the early years of the French and Indian War.

In 1755, Great Britain sent troops to America to protect settlers along the northern and western frontiers of the colonies that bordered French lands. As the French and Indian War went on, Connecticut assembled the largest fighting force in its history. Starting in 1755, more than 3,000 men were sent to fight along the New York frontier, and in 1760, more Connecticut troops went into Canada. Almost 30,000 Connecticut men joined the militia during the war, though not all of them actually fought the enemy.

Eliasaph Preston of Wallingford, Connecticut, wrote this letter to his mother in 1759 while he was fighting with the British Army at Crown Point, New York, during the French and Indian War. The British marched from this site to capture Fort Ticonderoga.

Albany June ye first Day 1759 Ever
Honoured father & Mother after My duty to you
and my Love to my Brothers & Sisters is Presented
I would Let you know my Circum Stances a Little
I am at Present in a Comfortable State of health for
which I bless god: yesterday I arrived at this Place:
My journey has been Long and tedious but through
ye Mercy of god I have got pretty well over it; we
are Encamped on ye west Side of the River on the
Hill: the army in general is very healthy: there is a
few Sick with ye Meazles but None with any
other Distemper: Last Tuesday a Rhodeisland
in this Place
... to Death: and I hear there is an

BATTLEFRONT REPORT

In 1758, a New Hampshire newspaper gave this detailed account of the wounds suffered by one Connecticut soldier fighting in New York:

> *. . . the enemy fired upon [Lieutenant Wooster], 8 bullets lodged in him, 3 of which are taken out; he had also three wounds by a tomahawk, two of which were on his head, and the other in his elbow. . . . He was sensible all the while the enemy were scalping him, and finding him wounded in so many places he could not run, and the enemy close upon him, he fell on his face and feigned himself dead, and no doubt but the enemy thought he actually was; however they gave him two blows on his head, but not so hard as to deprive him of his senses.*

The fighting in North America ended in 1760, with a British victory at Montreal, Canada. The war was officially over in 1763 with the signing of the Treaty of Paris. With its victory, Great Britain took control of all of France's territory on mainland North America. For Connecticut and the rest of New England, the threat of French invasion was gone for good.

A Slowly Growing Colony

COMMERCE AND EDUCATION *increase in importance as farmland becomes scarce. Women gain a foothold in business and politics.*

Throughout the 18th century, farming remained a way of life for most Connecticut residents, but land along the rivers and Long Island Sound became more expensive, if it was available for sale at all. Some Connecticut men left the colony to find land they could afford, while others headed to the remote eastern and western hills of the colony.

OPPOSITE: A hilltop view of New London, Connecticut, shows the stone walls found throughout the New England colonies and the city's harbor in the distance.

Compared to the fertile valleys, growing crops was hard in the hills, where the soil was rocky. Many farmers switched from growing crops to raising livestock, which grazed on grasses that grew fairly easily on the hillsides. In the valleys, farmers tended to raise grains, and Wethersfield became famous for its red onions. More than ever before, Connecticut farmers produced more food than local residents needed, so they traded their extra for such goods as molasses, sugar, tobacco, and manufactured products.

STONE WALLS

THE ROCKY LAND OF THE CONNECTICUT HILLS PRESENTED an ongoing problem that farmers throughout New England had faced for more than a century. The many rocks and stones had to cleared before crops could be planted. Each spring, new rocks appeared on the surface, pushed up from underground by the freezing and thawing of the land. In the 17th century, Connecticut farmers often just dumped the rocks in a pile. Over time, the landowners used the rocks and stones to build walls that marked their property lines. Stone walls are still common today in Connecticut, though many of them are being torn down as farmland is developed for housing and businesses. In 2002, University of Connecticut professor Robert Thorson started the Stone Wall Initiative, to educate people about the history of Connecticut's stone walls and to try to preserve remaining walls. In 2005, he continued this effort in his book *Exploring Stone Walls*.

In an effort to expand beyond Connecticut's crowded borders, some investors turned to the colony's charter. The 1662 document said that Connecticut extended to the Pacific Ocean. When that was written, the colony of Pennsylvania did not exist, but by 1753, that colony included some of the land that technically belonged to Connecticut. That year the Connecticut investors set up the Susquehannah Company to buy and settle land that was now claimed by Pennsylvania. In 1755, the Connecticut General Assembly approved the company's plan to obtain a royal charter. The French and Indian War delayed settlement of the Susquehannah Company lands, and the first settlers who arrived in 1763 were attacked by local Indians. The Connecticut newcomers also battled Pennsylvanians who resisted this invasion of what they considered their land. The fighting was called the Yankee-Pennamite War.

In October 1773, the General Assembly declared that the Connecticut settlers formed *"a distinct town, with like powers and privileges as other towns in [Connecticut] by law have . . . and shall be called by the name Westmoreland."* Pennsylvania, however, always asserted its claim to the area, and after the American Revolution it won a legal battle to keep it. Former Connecticut residents remained in the state and, after one more armed conflict with local Pennsylvanians, won the right to keep their lands.

Ways to Wealth

Although farming remained important in Connecticut, increasing numbers of colonists developed new skills. Clockmakers, tinsmiths, and gunmakers all became popular trades. Fishermen sailed from ports along Long Island Sound, and the colony was well known for its oysters. Merchants and ship captains also became more common, as they transported the extra food produced on Connecticut farms and traded it in Boston and New York for manufactured goods from England. These goods included clothes, kitchen dishes and utensils, and books. Some Connecticut goods were also directly traded with the West Indies, in return for sugar and molasses. Molasses was frequently used to make rum, a popular drink in 18th-century New England. Trade with the West Indies was illegal, but Connecticut sea captains smuggled goods in order to get around those restrictions and to avoid paying taxes on the goods they carried.

smuggle—to bring goods into a place illegally

Connecticut sea captains and merchants did not play a large role in the slave trade. But Connecticut residents did make money trading their goods with the sugar plantations in the West Indies, where many slaves worked. By 1775, the slave population of Connecticut was small compared to that in southern colonies. Still, with slightly more than 6,400 slaves, Connecticut had more than any other New England colony.

This portrait of Elijah Boardman, a merchant who ran a dry-goods (textiles and clothing) store in Connecticut, was painted by Ralph Earl in 1789 and now hangs in the Metropolitan Museum of Art in New York City.

Connecticut's centers of trade—and largest cities—remained the cities and towns located along rivers and Long Island Sound. In 1756, Middletown, south of Hartford on the Connecticut River, had the largest population, with slightly more than 5,600 people. (By this time, the population of the entire colony was about 130,000.) The river was deeper there than farther north, so larger ships that could not reach Hartford unloaded their cargoes in Middletown. Norwich, on the Thames, was second with about 5,500. New London remained the major port for overseas trade. Smaller towns such as Windham and Lebanon served as trade centers for local farmers. From there, merchants brought the goods to the colony's major ports. Starting in the 1730s, a new source of money for Connecticut came from the earth. Large amounts of iron ore were discovered in the northwest corner of the colony. Stone furnaces turned the ore into iron, which was then used to make cannon, anchors, and other items. The town of Salisbury became the heart of the colony's iron industry. Salisbury iron was considered the best in the American colonies because of its strength.

New England's Largest Plantation

Large plantations worked by many slaves historically are associated with the southern United States. But in 2001, Connecticut archaeologists Jerry Sawyer and Warren Perry announced their discovery of a large plantation in Salem. During the 18th century, Samuel Browne of Rhode Island owned some 4,000 acres (1,620 ha) of land in Connecticut. Browne hired overseers to run his plantation, which used at least 60 slaves to produce meat, lumber, and grain. That was more than twice as many slaves as lived on the only other Connecticut plantation, and more than on plantations in southern Rhode Island, the only other New England colony with large plantations.

A portrait of the future governor of Connecticut Jonathan Trumbull and his wife, Faith, dressed in fine clothing befitting Trumbull's status as a successful merchant.

Society in the 18th Century

In the towns and cities, men in certain professions tended to own the most property and control politics. These included ministers, officers of the militia, and wealthy farmers and merchants. Some of the leaders were doctors and lawyers. These professions grew as the colony sent more young men to college and the demand for their services increased. Unskilled laborers, sailors, and slaves performed the hardest work in the trade centers. In some villages away from the river valleys, the land was not rich enough for most farmers to produce extra crops for market. Few were able to achieve great wealth. The sons of small farmers knew their best chance to better themselves and find a career was in the large towns.

The Changing Lives of Women

Women throughout the Colonies saw changes, both good and bad, as Connecticut moved into the 18th century. During the 17th century, women were allowed to bring legal complaints against others. Typical cases included women defending their honor against public insults or trying to collect money they were owed. By the 18th century, however, lawyers were part of the legal system in Connecticut. They were all men, and they often shut women out of the courts. Women still could not vote, hold public office, or serve on juries.

Still, the General Assembly did offer women some legal protection. In the early years of the colony, a husband had full control of land owned by his wife before their marriage. After 1723, a woman had to approve any dealings her husband made with her property.

Women were also more involved in economic affairs during the 18th century. As before, they helped their husbands run family businesses, and they might take over the work completely when their husbands died. Women also worked independently in such areas as teaching, weaving, dressmaking, and retailing. Dressmaker Betty Foot of Colchester noted in her diary of 1775, "*I went to Mr. Amos Wells's to work and Mrs. Wells and I made two gowns for her little girls. . . .*"

A COLONIAL DIARY

BETTY FOOT KEPT HER DIARY FOR LESS THAN ONE YEAR. During that time, she noted her work schedule and daily events. For one busy day she wrote, "*I went to Sally Wells's funeral and at night Ellen [her cousin] was married to David Wilds.*" Foot also recorded a poem that she wrote in her diary. Here is part of it:

O hark o hark a little while
I'll sing a ditty shall make you smile
Tis of a merchants son of late
As he came sailing up the straight.

More chances to make money gave 18th-century Connecticut women some independence. In general, however, men assumed that women were not equal to men.

A woman teacher received less salary than a man, and fathers and husbands expected their wives and daughters to obey them. Women, for the most part, still centered their lives on taking care of their families and working in the home.

Intellectual Life

During the 18th century, the education system improved. Better schooling was one reason why women played a slightly larger role in the economy. The wealthiest and best-educated parents had the best-schooled children. Samuel Peters, a Connecticut writer of the 1700s, claimed that some Connecticut women *"will freely talk upon the subject of history, geography, and mathematics . . . . and I have known not a few of them so well skilled in Greek and Latin as often to [embarrass] learned gentlemen."*

The desire to improve education applied to the colony's Indians as well. In 1743, a minister named Eleazar Wheelock, from Lebanon, allowed a Mohegan named Samson Occom to attend a school Wheelock ran. Occom's intellectual skills impressed the minister, who later opened a school just for Indians. Wheelock hoped the students would return to their tribes to convert the Indians to Christianity and teach them to read and write. Wheelock later moved his school to New Hampshire and stopped admitting Indians. The school became Dartmouth College.

PROFILE

Samson Occom

Next to the sachem Uncas, Samson Occom (1723–1792) was the most famous Mohegan in colonial Connecticut. In 1741, during the Great Awakening, Occom heard the preaching of a traveling minister and became a Christian. After leaving Eleazar Wheelock's school, Occom became a minister and a teacher. For a time during the 1760s, he traveled through Great Britain, raising money for Wheelock's Indian school. People there sometimes stared at him or made fun of him. They were shocked to see an Indian who could read and preach about Christ. Occom later wrote to Wheelock, *"I was quite willing to become a . . . laughing stock, in strange countries to promote your cause."* Later, however, Occom saw that Americans were relentless in their efforts to control all Indian land. Angry at white society, Occom started a community called Brothertown in western New York. He wanted Christian Indians of southern New England to live there as brothers, far from white settlements. After Occom's death, the Brothertown settlers moved to Wisconsin.

Connecticut did not share any borders with French territory (see inset map), yet it helped the British win the French and Indian War by sending thousands of troops to fight. One conflict that was not settled until after the Colonies gained their independence from Britain was between Connecticut and Pennsylvania over a tract of land called Westmoreland (green area on map). Pennsylvania eventually won this battle, but settlers from Connecticut were allowed to keep their lands.

The increase in education helped Connecticut publishers by enlarging the number of customers who could read their newspapers. New Haven's *Connecticut Gazette* was the colony's first paper, appearing in 1755. Within several decades, every major city had its own weekly paper. Hartford's first paper, the *Connecticut Courant,* which appeared in 1764, promised to be "*useful and entertaining, not only as a channel for news, but assisting to all those who may have occasion to make use of it as an advertiser.*" Today called the *Hartford Courant,* it is the oldest continuously published newspaper in the United States.

CHAPTER EIGHT

Revolutionary Connecticut

CONNECTICUT RESIDENTS *generally support the Patriots in Massachusetts. Connecticut Governor Jonathan Trumbull readies the militia to aid the rebels in Boston and defend Connecticut Colony from the British. The Salisbury iron mines provide ore for cannon during the war.*

Great Britain's victory in the French and Indian War vastly expanded its empire. To pay its war debts and build forts in the former French lands it now controlled, the British government needed money. In 1764, Parliament passed the Sugar Act, which taxed sugar and molasses coming into the Colonies. It also taxed other imported items, such as wine and expensive cloth.

OPPOSITE: During the Battle of Breed's (Bunker) Hill, General Israel Putnam rides toward the front lines, with Redcoats trailing him, to ready his troops. General Putnam's bravery throughout the battle encouraged his troops to fight and eventually defeat the British.

Protesting Taxes

Some American merchants and politicians protested the Sugar Act. Connecticut's leaders did not like the new law, but were more concerned about Parliament's plan to tax paper used for public documents, including sermons, legal papers, newspapers, and even playing cards. The proposed law, called the Stamp Act, seemed to interfere with the internal governing of the Colonies. Connecticut leaders saw the new tax as an attack on their freedoms, as spelled out in the colony's charter of 1662.

Governor Thomas Fitch disliked the Stamp Act, which Parliament passed in 1765. Still, he said he would enforce the new law so that the British would not take even stronger steps that threatened Connecticut's charter. If he disobeyed, he said, "*the King . . . would deprive the people of the privilege of electing [the governor and council]; and then the whole charter would be at once struck up.*"

Newspapers in Connecticut protested the act, and ministers spoke out against it in churches. Some Connecticut men who opposed the tax joined the Sons of Liberty. This group actively fought British policies in the years before the American Revolution. Several other Colonies had their own Sons of Liberty groups.

Colonists everywhere began to boycott British goods. British merchants who

boycott—an agreement made by a group of people to refuse to purchase goods from a nation or company

traded with the Colonies began to lose money. They pressured Parliament to repeal the Stamp Act, and Parliament finally agreed. But British lawmakers said that they still had the right to collect other taxes.

For the next several years, Connecticut's relationship with Great Britain was fairly smooth. Few residents protested the Townshend Acts of 1767, which placed taxes on tea, paper, and other items brought into the Colonies. In Boston, however, protests against the Townshend Acts were stronger, and in 1768 the British sent troops to the city to keep order. By 1769, some merchants in eastern Connecticut were joining a new boycott that had begun in Massachusetts. The boycott, however, ended in 1770, when the British removed the taxes on all imported goods, except for tea.

The Road to War

In 1773, Boston residents boarded three British ships and threw 342 chests of tea into Boston Harbor. These Patriots were protesting the tea tax and British policies in general. Parliament responded the next year to the Patriots' "Boston Tea Party" with a series of laws that the Americans called the Intolerable Acts. The laws closed down the port of Boston and put Massachusetts under a military governor appointed by the king. Connecticut's lawmakers said that these new laws were a further threat to the rights of all

Americans. In May 1774, the Sons of Liberty in Farmington declared that *"the present [British government], being instigated by the devil and led on by their wicked and corrupt hearts, have a design to take away our liberties and properties and to enslave us forever."*

In September, all the Colonies except Georgia sent delegates to a meeting in Philadelphia. At this First Continental Congress, the delegates declared loyalty to the king. But, they declared, Parliament did not have the right to tax the American colonies or control their politics without their approval.

delegate—a person chosen to speak or act for others

As 1775 began, the Massachusetts Patriots set up their own government, which was illegal, and gathered weapons. On April 19, General Thomas Gage, the military governor of Massachusetts, sent troops to Concord to seize weapons and supplies stored there. In Lexington, Patriot militia waited for them, and the two sides exchanged shots. More fighting took place in Concord. These encounters marked the beginning of the American Revolution.

News of the fighting quickly reached Connecticut. Governor Jonathan Trumbull met with the General Assembly to create an army. Of all the colonial governors of the time, Trumbull was the only one who openly supported the Patriots in Massachusetts. He sent a letter to General Gage saying that *"outrages have been committed as would disgrace even barbarians,"* and Trumbull warned that Connecticut was ready to defend itself.

PROFILE

Jonathan Trumbull

Jonathan Trumbull was born in Lebanon, Connecticut, in 1710. After attending Harvard University, he became a successful merchant and the owner of the largest meat-packing business in the colony.

Trumbull began his 50-year career in public service as Deputy from Lebanon to the General Assembly. During the Revolutionary War, he planned cattle drives from Hartford to Pennsylvania to provide the Continental Army with meat and other provisions during the long winter at Valley Forge. His friend, George Washington, called Trumbull "Brother Jonathan" for his good works. Industry within the state exploded during the Revolution as Trumbull encouraged manufacturing that served the war needs, earning Connecticut the name the "Provision State." He was elected governor in 1769, an office he would hold for 14 years. Trumbull died in 1785 with less popularity than during the war years, but he was still considered a great Patriot.

Meanwhile, Connecticut militia rushed to Boston to help the Patriots there. One of the first volunteers was Benedict Arnold of New Haven. Massachusetts officials asked Arnold to lead a force against the British fort in Ticonderoga, New York. At the same time, Trumbull ordered Ethan Allen to take the fort. Allen was a Connecticut native who had moved to Vermont, which was then part of New Hampshire. Allen led a group of soldiers known as the Green Mountain Boys. Allen and Arnold worked together to take the fort, giving the Americans their first major victory of the Revolution.

Ethan Allen and the Green Mountain Boys surprised the British guards on duty at Fort Ticonderoga at dawn on May 9, 1775. The guards quickly fled their posts. Allen, along with Benedict Arnold, broke through the door to the quarters of the officers in charge and demanded their surrender. Only one shot was fired by a British guard, but there were no injuries.

The War Years in Connecticut

In June 1775, Connecticut forces fought bravely at the Battle of Breed's (Bunker) Hill, just outside Boston in Charlestown. General Israel Putnam had led the call to build a fort on Breed's Hill, where most of the fighting took place. Connecticut men also took part in the siege of Boston, which was led by the new American commander in chief, General George Washington. In the years to come, many Connecticut soldiers fought bravely at battles across the Colonies. These soldiers included African-American slaves and free blacks, as well as Native Americans. In some towns, almost ten percent of the militia members were African American, and they also served on Connecticut ships. Some slaves were given their freedom in return for their military service.

BATTLEFRONT AND HOME FRONT

Less than one week after the fighting in Lexington and Concord, Connecticut resident Nathan Peters was in Massachusetts to help the Patriots. He often exchanged letters with his wife, Lois, who remained behind in Preston. Here is part of one of her letters to him, written after the Battle of Breed's (Bunker) Hill.

Dear Husband *June 20*

. . . We have heard of the battle you have had among you but we hear so many stories we know not what to believe . . . our fears are many but we hope for the best. My heart aches for you and all our friends there but I keep up as good spirits as possible . . . our corn looks well and work goes on as well as I could wish . . . wishing you the best of heaven's blessings and hope that God in due time will return you to your family in safety.

After the siege forced the British to leave Boston in March 1776, most of the fighting shifted to the Middle Colonies of New York, New Jersey, and Pennsylvania and then to the south. Still, Connecticut residents living along Long Island Sound feared British raids. In 1777, the British raided Danbury, where the Patriots had a warehouse. On their retreat, the British suffered heavy losses near Ridgefield, where General Benedict Arnold led the American forces. Two years later, British warships entered New Haven harbor and took the city. The last major attack came in 1781. A dozen ships and more than a hundred buildings were burned in a raid on New London and Groton, led by traitor Benedict Arnold.

siege—a military tactic in which one army surrounds another, cutting off food and supplies in order to force a surrender

During the Revolution, Connecticut played an important role in supplying weapons for the Patriot cause. As early as June 1775, ads went up across the colony seeking skilled craftsmen. One ad in Windham County called for *"any gunsmith or lock-maker . . . willing to supply the colony with any number of fire arms."* In Litchfield County, the iron ore of Salisbury was used to produce 80 percent of the American cannon used during the war. Connecticut soon earned the nickname "the arsenal of the Revolution."

arsenal—a place where weapons are made or stored

Connecticut also provided political leaders during the war. Silas Deane was one of Connecticut's delegates at the Second Continental Congress. In 1776, he was sent to France to try to win French aid against the British. That year, four Connecticut leaders signed the Declaration of Independence: Roger Sherman, Oliver Wolcott, Samuel Huntington, and William Williams. In Hartford, Governor Trumbull played a key role in supplying Washington's army with food, clothing, and weapons. So did businessman Jeremiah Wadsworth.

Sybil Ludington

SIXTEEN-YEAR-OLD SYBIL LUDINGTON, THE DAUGHTER OF A colonel in the Fredericksburg, New York, militia, became a hero of the Revolutionary Waron April 26, 1777, when she helped her father muster his men to aid the colonists of Connecticut. Late that evening word came to her home that the British were burning the town of Danbury, a food and ammunition depot for the Patriots, only 25 miles from the New York border. Colonel Ludington made a difficult decision in order to stop the Redcoats from continuing on through Connecticut. He sent his daughter Sybil to muster his men scattered throughout the Putnam County region, while he stayed behind to organize his troops upon their arrival. Sybil rode her horse, Star, more than 20 miles through the night from farmhouse to farmhouse alerting the men that the Connecticut militia needed their help. By the time she returned home early that morning, more than 400 men were ready to fight the Battle of Ridgefield and drive the Redcoats back towards Long Island Sound.

Underwater Warfare

As a student at Yale, Connecticut native David Bushnell developed mines designed to explode underwater. When the American Revolution began, he designed a submarine that allowed sailors to attach an explosive to the bottom of a British warship. The egg-shaped vessel he built was later called the *Turtle*. It was the world's first military submarine. A pilot inside powered the sub with two oars. One oar moved the *Turtle* forward and backward, and another moved it up and down. The *Turtle* went into combat on September 6, 1776, in New York harbor. The pilot, however, could not attach the mine correctly, and the mission failed. The British later destroyed the sub, but Bushnell continued to build mines that were used to attack British ships.

After the War

In October 1781, General Washington's forces, with crucial aid from France, defeated the British at Yorktown, Virginia. With that loss, Parliament lost its will to fight, and peace talks began in 1782. The war officially ended in 1783 with the signing of the Treaty of Paris. The American colonies were now officially recognized as the United States of America. The country had a national government created by a document called the Articles of Confederation.

Over time, some Americans saw problems with the Articles of Confederation. The states sometimes argued with each other, and the national government was too weak to settle their disputes. Through the summer of 1787, delegates from every state except Rhode Island met in

Philadelphia to strengthen the Articles of Confederation. In the end, they created a whole new government, as outlined in a new document, the U.S. Constitution.

Connecticut's delegates to this Constitutional Convention were Oliver Ellsworth, William S. Johnson, and Roger Sherman. During the convention, Sherman helped settle a dispute by proposing what was called the Connecticut—or Great—Compromise. The delegates disagreed about how many representatives each state would have in Congress, the lawmaking branch of the new government. Large states wanted the number based on population, which would give them more members—and more power—than small states. The small states, including Connecticut, opposed this plan. Sherman suggested that in one house of Congress membership would be based on population. In the other, each state would have an equal number of representatives. The delegates accepted the compromise and completed the Constitution in September. Before it could go into effect, nine states had to ratify, or approve, it. On January 8, 1788, Connecticut became the fifth state to ratify the Constitution. Although a small state, Connecticut played a big role in building the value of self-rule that Americans still cherish today.

Roger Sherman

Time Line

1614 Dutch trader Adriaen Block explores the Connecticut River as far north as Enfield.

1631 Wahginnacut, sachem of the Wongunk Indians, invites Massachusetts Bay settlers to live along the Connecticut River.

1632 Edward Winslow of Plymouth Colony explores the Connecticut River.

1633 The Dutch build a fort called *Huys de Hoop* (House of Good Hope) at what is now Hartford; English settlers from Plymouth build a trading post at what is now Windsor.

1634 John Oldham leads settlers from Massachusetts Bay to what is now Wethersfield.

1636 Thomas Hooker and Samuel Stone lead settlers from Massachusetts Bay to Hartford.

1637 Connecticut settlers defeat the Pequot Indians in the Pequot War.

1638 John Davenport leads settlers to New Haven.

1639 The river towns of Windsor, Hartford, and Wethersfield create the Fundamental Orders, outlining a system of government for the River Colony.

1643 New Haven and the River Colony join with Massachusetts Bay and Plymouth to create the New England Confederation.

1647 Alse Young of Windsor is executed for being a witch.

1661–1663 Witch trials in Hartford

1662 John Winthrop, Jr., receives a charter from King Charles II that formally creates Connecticut Colony.

1665 New Haven joins Connecticut Colony.

1675 Connecticut troops take part in King Philip's War, the last major Indian war in southern New England.

1686 The Dominion of New England is formed.

1687 Edmund Andros, governor of the Dominion of New England, demands but does not get Connecticut's charter.

1689 After England's Glorious Revolution of 1688, Andros is removed from power and Connecticut resumes its old government under the 1662 charter.

1701 New Haven becomes a co-capital of the colony with Hartford; Yale College is founded in Saybrook and later moves to New Haven.

1741 During the Great Awakening, Connecticut-born minister Jonathan Edwards gives one of the most famous sermons of the era at an Enfield meetinghouse.

1745 Connecticut forces help seize the French fort of Louisbourg on Cape Breton Island, north of Nova Scotia.

1753 A group of investors form the Susquehannah Company to settle lands that Connecticut claims in Pennsylvania.

1755 Connecticut troops are sent to fight in New York during the French and Indian War; the *Connecticut Gazette* becomes the first newspaper in the colony.

1774 Connecticut Patriots speak out against the Intolerable Acts.

1775 The American Revolution begins in Massachusetts; Connecticut natives Ethan Allen and Benedict Arnold seize Fort Ticonderoga from the British.

1776 David Bushnell builds the world's first military submarine.

1777 British troops raid Danbury, and Benedict Arnold attacks the retreating British forces at Ridgefield.

1781 Traitor Benedict Arnold leads a destructive raid against New London; a U.S. victory at Yorktown, Virginia, signals the end of the Revolution.

1787 At the Constitutional Convention in Philadelphia, Roger Sherman proposes the Connecticut Compromise.

1788 Connecticut becomes the fifth state to ratify the U.S. Constitution.

Resources

BOOKS

Bullock, Steven C. *The American Revolution: A History in Documents*. New York: Oxford University Press, 2003.

Malaspina, Ann. *A Primary Source History of the Colony of Connecticut*. New York: Rosen Central Primary Source, 2006.

Newman, Shirlee Petkin. *The Pequots*. New York: Franklin Watts, 2000.

Slavicek, Louise Chipley. *Life Among the Puritans*. San Diego: Lucent, 2001.

Sonneborn, Liz. *Benedict Arnold: Hero and Traitor*. Philadelphia: Chelsea House, 2006.

Wiener, Roberta. *Connecticut: The History of Connecticut Colony*. Chicago: Raintree, 2005.

Wood, Peter. *Strange New Land: African Americans, 1617–1776*. New York: Oxford University Press, 1996.

WEB SITES

Colonial Connecticut Records
http://www.colonialct.uconn.edu/
From the University of Connecticut, an electronic version of the records of the General Assembly from 1636 to 1776.

A Colonial Family and Community
http://www.hfmgv.org/education/smartfun/colonial/intro/intro.html
This Web site traces the life of a real 18th-century Connecticut family, using records from the father's business.

Connecticut History on the Web
http://www.connhistory.org/arch_contents.htm
This site includes primary sources on the Pequot War and later periods of Connecticut history.

Mashantucket Pequot Museum and Research Center
http://www.pequotmuseum.org/
The Pequot provide a detailed look at their tribal history through the museum's Web site.

The Society of Colonial Wars in the State of Connecticut
http://www.colonialwarsct.org/index.htm
The society provides a detailed time line of events in Connecticut from 1614 to 1775.

A Struggle from the Start: Objects in the Dark
http://www.hartford-hwp.com/HBHP/exhibit/menu.html
From the Hartford Black History Project, this section of an online exhibit traces the history of slavery in Connecticut during colonial times.

Quote Sources

CHAPTER ONE

p. 14 "The natives…their enemies." http://www.colonialwarsct.org/1614.htm; "Connittekock is…the countryside." http://www.nnp.org/annals/2001.pdf#xml=http://search.atomz.com/search/pdfhelper.tk?sp_o=12,100000,0; p. 19 "everyone but…great friendship." http://rs6.loc.gov/cgi-bin/query/r?intldl/awkb:@field(DOCID+@lit(gckb026_0001)); "was very desirous…skins of beaver." Bemer, Francis J. *John Winthrop: America's Forgotten Founding Father.* New York: Oxford University Press, 2003, p. 265; p. 20 "Up the river to trade," www.colonialwarsct.org/1633.htm; "I must obey my commands." www.colonialwarsct.org/1633.htm; p. 21 "the King of…build there." Winthrop, John. *The Journal of John Winthrop, 1630–1649.* Abridged edition. Dunn, Richard S. and Laetitia Yeandle, editors. Cambridge: The Belknap Press of Harvard University, 1996, p. 57.

CHAPTER TWO

p. 26 "God makes…there be safe." http://www.puritansermons.com/banner/murray5.htm; p. 28 "expose [the Newtown…the Indians." http://www.puritansermons.com/banner/murray5.htm; "About 60…arrived safe there." Winthrop, John. *The Journal of John Winthrop, 1630–1649.* Abridged edition. Dunn, Richard S. and Laetitia Yeandle, editors. Cambridge: The Belknap Press of Harvard University, 1996, p. 85; p. 30 "We are Pequots…and children." Oberg, Michael Leroy. *Uncas First of the Mohegans.* Ithaca, New York: Cornell University Press, 2003, p. 56; "there shall…the Pequot." Oberg, p. 58; p. 33 "When [the fire]…rejoicing of ourselves." http://bc.barnard.columbia.edu/~rmccaugh/early AC/readings/pequot/pequot.pdf; "eleven coats…the English manner." Calder, Isabel MacBeath. *The New Haven Colony.* Reprint. Hamden, CT: Archon Books, 1970, p. 54; p. 35 "the foundation…of the people." Miller, Perry, editor. The American Puritans. Garden City, NY: Anchor, 1956, p. 89; "the blessed…of God." Miller, p. 89; "maintain and preserve…lord Jesus." Taylor, Robert J. *Colonial Connecticut: A History.* Millwood, NY: KTO Press, 1979, p. 20.

CHAPTER THREE

p. 38 "all manner…merchandise whatsoever." Bushman, Richard L. *From Puritan to Yankee: Character and the Social Order in Connecticut, 1690–1765.* Cambridge: Harvard University Press, 1967, p. 26; p. 39 "the great…blood of the [strongest]." Smith, Helen Everston. *Colonial Days and Ways As Gathered From Family Papers.* Reprint. New York: Frederick Unger Publishing, 1966, p. 50; p. 40 "to bake…no offenset." Calder, Isabel MacBeath. *The New Haven Colony.* Reprint. Hamden, CT: Archon Books, 1970, p.156; p. 41 "It was believed…heard of after." http://www.nhharbor.net/articles/Great%20Ship%20and%20Phantom%20Ship-1/index.htm; p. 42 "If any man…put to death." http://www.connhistory.org/col_reading.htm#laws; "conspire or…against the [government]." http://www.connhistory.org/col_reading.htm#laws; "it was [then]…may not escape." Andrus, Silas, editor. *The Blue Laws: The Earliest Laws of Connecticut and New Haven Colonies.* Reprint. Storrs, CT: Bibliopola Press, 1999, p. 103; p. 43 "Help me,…upon me…." St. George, Robert Blair. *Conversing by Signs: Poetics of Implication in Colonial New England Culture.* Chapel Hill, NC: University of North Carolian Press, 1998, p. 116; "…we have not…and orderly…." http://rootsweb.com/~ctfairfi/stamford/witch_trial1.htm; p. 45 "so much learning… capital laws." http://www.connhistory.org/col_reading.htm#laws; "in some honest…[the colony]." http://www.connhistory.org /col_reading.htm#laws.

CHAPTER FOUR

p. 48 "a general combination…all the plantations." Calder, Isabel MacBeath. *The New Haven Colony.* Reprint. Hamden, CT: Archon Books, 1970, p.156; p. 49 "excellent harbor… future trade." http://newlondongazette.com/name.html; "a ship of…a biscuit ashore." Van Dusen, Albert E. *Puritans Against the Wilderness: Connecticut History to 1763.* Chester, CT: Pequot Press, 1975, p. 13; p. 51 "That for the…said company." http://www.law.ou.edu/us history/colony.shtml; p. 54 "…that the constable…English with them." http://www.colonialct.uconn.edu/NewCTScanImages/0016THEP/V0002/I000/03800376.jpg; p. 57 "The good people…than to oppose." http://www.colonialct.uconn.edu/NewCTScanImages/0017THEP/V0003/I000/04810465.jpg.

CHAPTER FIVE

p. 59 "There are…above 30." Taylor, Robert J. *Colonial Connecticut: A History.* Millwood, NY: KTO Press, 1979, p. 34; p. 60 "no servant…corporal [physical] punishment." Andrus, Silas, editor. *The Blue Laws: The Earliest Laws of Connecticut and New Haven Colonies.* Reprint. Storrs, CT: Bibliopola Press, 1999, p. 103; p. 65; "convenient time…and rest." Andrus, p. 66; pp. 60–61 "hard labor…severe punishment." Taylor, p. 157; p. 61 "one hundred eighty…as servants." "Complicity: How Connecticut Chained Itself to Slavery." *Northeast Magazine* special issue. *Hartford Courant,* September 29, 2002, p. 24; p. 63 "shall be liable…month's imprisonment." http://www.colonialct.uconn.edu/ViewPageBySequentialID.cfm?v=02&p=313&c=4&StartVolume=1&StartPage=1; p. 64 "often quarreling…of the peace." http://www.colonialct.uconn.edu/ViewPageBySequentialID.cfm?v=02&p=313&c=4&StartVolume=1&StartPage=1; pp. 64–65 "that if any negro…for one offense." http://www.colonialct.uconn.edu/ViewPageBySequentialID.cfm?v=02&p=313&c=4&StartVolume=1&StartPage=1; p. 65 "having heard…[the master's] fault." Knight, Sarah Kemble. *The Journal of Madam Knight.* Boston: David R. Godine, 1972, p. 21; "named Nero,…five dollars reward." Van Dusen, Albert E. *Puritans Against the Wilderness: Connecticut History to 1763.* Chester, CT: Pequot Press, 1975, p. 100; p. 67 "my mistress…devouring fire." "Complicity: How Connecticut Chained Itself to Slavery." *Northeast Magazine* special issue. *Hartford Courant,* September 29, 2002, p. 15.

CHAPTER SIX

p. 70 "youth may be…civil state." http://www.yale.edu/about/history/html; p. 71 "a steady stream…of their souls." Taylor, Robert J. *Colonial Connecticut: A History.* Millwood, NY: KTO Press, 1979, p. 133; p. 72 "Your wickedness…bottomless gulf." *Annals of America, Volume I.* Chicago: Encyclopedia Britannica, 1968; p. 427; p. 73 "It was difficult…inconsistence of it." Campisi, Jack, editor. *Eighteenth Century Native Communities of Southern New England in the Colonial Context.* Mashantucket, CT: Mashantucket Pequot Museum and Research Center, 2005, p. 24; p. 74 "can expect no…subdued." Selesky, Harold. *War and Society in Colonial Connecticut.* New Haven: Yale University Press, 1990, p. 75; p. 77 "…the enemy fired…of his senses." http://www.earlyamerica.com/review/1998/scalping.html.

CHAPTER SEVEN

p. 81 "a distinct town…name Westmoreland." http://www.colonialct.uconn.edu/NewCTScanImages/0028THEP/V0014/I000/02220218.jpg; p. 87 "I went to…her little girls…" Ulrich, Laurel Thatcher. *The Age of Homespun: Objects and Stories in the Creation of American Myth.* New York: Alfred A. Knopf, 2000, p. 219; "I went to…David Wilds." Ulrich, 213; "O hark…up the straight." Ulrich, p. 217; p. 88 "will freely…learned gentlemen." Taylor, Robert J. *Colonial Connecticut: A History.* Millwood, NY: KTO Press, 1979, p. 169; p. 89 "I was quite…promote your cause." http://www.common-place.org/vol-04/no-04/brooks/2.shtml; p. 91 "useful and entertaining…an advertiser." Smith, J. Eugene. *One Hundred Years of Hartford's Courant: From Colonial Times through the Civil War.* Reprint. Hamden, CT: Archon Books, 1970, p. 3.

CHAPTER EIGHT

p. 94 "the King…struck up." Selesky, Harold. *War and Society in Colonial Connecticut.* New Haven: Yale University Press, 1990, p. 223; p. 96 "the present…enslave us forever." Commager, Henry Steele, and Richard B. Morris., editors. *The Spirit of 'Seventy-Six.* New York: Harper & Row, 1967, p. 21; "outrages…even barbarians." Taylor, Robert J. *Colonial Connecticut: A History.* Millwood, NY: KTO Press, 1979, p. 241; p. 99 "Dear Husband…family in safety." Guthman, William H., ed. *The Correspondence of Captain Nathan and Lois Peters.* Hartford: The Connecticut Historical Society, 1980, pp. 11–12; p. 100 "any gunsmith…fire arms." Ketchum, Richard M. *Decisive Day: The Battle for Bunker Hill.* Garden City, NY: Doubleday & Company, 1974, p. 63.

INDEX

About the Author and Consultant

MICHAEL BURGAN has been writing about colonial and Revolutionary-era America, immigration, religion, famous Americans, sports, and many other subjects for children and young adults for more than ten years. His work has been published in *The New York Times*, *Sports Illustrated for Kids*, and by *National Geographic*. A former writer for Weekly Reader Corporation, Burgan has developed online resources and produced educational materials to be used by teachers in the classroom. Burgan is also the author of two other books in the *Voices from Colonial America* series: *New York* and *Massachusetts*. He lives in Chicago, Illinois.

BRENDAN MCCONVILLE is currently a professor in the Department of History at Boston University where he teaches courses on colonial America, the American Revolution, and American Politics. He received his Ph.D. from Brown University. McConville has written numerous books and articles on the early years of the American colonies. McConville is also the consultant for three other books in the *Voices from Colonial America* series: *Massachusetts*, *New Jersey*, and *Rhode Island*.

Illustration Credits

Cover, pages 12, 23, 48, 72, 78, 85, 103: Picture Collection, The Branch Libraries, The New York Public Library, Astor, Lenox and Tilden Foundation

Endsheets, pages 8, 43: Library of Congress

Title page, pages 11, 20, 24, 29, 31, 32, 36: The Granger Collection

Pages 8 (inset), 34, 90: National Geographic Society

Pages 9, 46, 70, 92, 98: North Wind Picture Archives

Pages 15, 55, 89: Connecticut Historical Society

Pages 18, 68: HIP/Art Resource, N.Y.

Pages 41, 51, 76: The New Haven Museum and Historical Society

Page 52: © Massachusetts Historical Society, Boston, MA, USA/The Bridgeman Art Library

Page 56: © Florence Griswold Museum, Old Lyme, Connecticut, USA/Gift of the Hartford Steam Boiler Inspection & Insurance Co./The Bridgeman Art Library

Page 58: Art Resource, N.Y.

Page 62: Connecticut State Library

Page 71: Connecticut State Archives

Page 75: State Historical Society of Wisconsin, Madison, USA,/The Bridgeman Art Library

Page 83: © The Metropolitan Museum of Art/Art Resource, NY

Page 102: OAR/National Undersea Research Program

NORTH AMERICA Divided into its III PRINCIPALL PARTS 1st ENGLISH Part Viz ENGLISH EMPIRE containi
N Foundland N Scotland N England N York N Jarsey Pensylvania Maryland Virginia Carolina Carolania or Florida California Sommer Is Bahama Is Jamaica &c Is CARIBY Is II SPANISH Pts viz N.